THE REWARDS
OF PUNISHMENT

THE REWARDS
OF PUNISHMENT
A Relational Theory of Norm Enforcement

Christine Horne

Stanford University Press
Stanford, California

Stanford University Press
Stanford, California

Printed in the United States of America on acid-free, archival-quality paper

Library of Congress Cataloging-in-Publication Data

Horne, Christine.

The rewards of punishment : a relational theory of norm enforcement /
Christine Horne.
    p.   cm.
Includes bibliographical references and index.
ISBN 978-0-8047-6021-8 (cloth : alk. paper) — ISBN
978-0-8047-6022-5 (pbk. : alk. paper)
    1. Social norms.   2. Interpersonal relations.   I. Title.
HM676.H67   2009
303.3'7—dc22   2008041878

Typeset by Westchester Book Group in 10/14 Minion

Contents

Preface

AS A STUDENT IN GRADUATE SCHOOL, I WAS INTERESTED IN the relation between law and the informal pressures exerted within communities. I soon realized that to understand the connection between the two—between rules enforced by the state and those maintained through interpersonal relationships—I needed to know something about norms. I needed to understand how they emerged and why they were enforced. I turned to the sociological literature but found few answers. The research across disciplines was equally messy. It contained many different ideas about what norms are, why they matter, and what we need to know about them.

I began to try to understand norms for myself. I focused on enforcement. This was partly because of my interest in the relation between law and norms and how investment in one might affect the other. It was partly because enforcement appeared to be the most tractable element of norms to get a handle on. And it was partly because I saw enforcement as crucial, both theoretically and practically. One might begin to study norms by trying to understand the emergence of particular rules. I chose not to start there, reasoning that whatever the rules were, if they were never enforced, they might not matter much.

I began developing my ideas and looking for a setting in which to test them. None of the settings I considered, however, gave me the kind of purchase on evaluating causal relations that I was looking for. In the midst of this search, I took a course on experimental methods and decided to take advantage of that opportunity to explore whether it would be possible to test my ideas in the lab. I discovered that it was.

Since then, I have continued to develop my understanding of norm enforcement and to use experimental methods to test theoretical predictions. This work has produced a series of journal articles. No single article tells the larger story. Each on its own is merely a small piece of the puzzle. In addition, the papers were written for experimentalists. Norms are important in a range of settings, however. Many people are interested in them—including those who do not do experimental work. I decided to write a book that would put together the pieces of the story in one place for a broad audience.

I describe the argument in nonformal ways, avoiding the use of technical language. I use concrete examples to illustrate the abstract ideas. The problem with examples is that they never perfectly match the theory and so are less precise than the theory itself. They are useful, however, for conveying the gist of an idea.

I also present the empirical support for the theory, including brief descriptions of the series of lab experiments that I conducted and their results. Readers who are interested in the methodological details can find them in the methods appendix and in the original published articles.

Finally, I explore some of the implications of the theory. While I believe that lab experiments are a powerful tool for testing causal explanations, I also believe that, for theory to be useful, it must shed light on substantive questions that people care about.

Michael Hechter encouraged me in this journey from the start. Michael is intensely curious and never takes the easy way out. His questions pushed me to develop my ideas in ways that I would not have done otherwise. I have appreciated his continual support, both in graduate school and since.

Linda Molm introduced me to experimental methods. She taught the graduate course in which I discovered that experiments might provide a useful tool—a way of testing the theoretical ideas I was developing. Since graduate school, I have benefited from my association with the Group Processes scholars in the American Sociological Association who furthered my education in both theory and experimental methods. I appreciate the many people who have provided intellectual insight, feedback, and personal and professional support along the way. I am indebted to Nobuyuki Takahashi for his patient programming assistance. And I am grateful to my research assistants—in particular, Chien-Fei Chen, Anna Cutlip, Karen Madden, Patience Payne, and Ben Scoll.

Larry and Gulsima sat through many conversations about the book. I appreciate their support for the project. Gulsima gave repeated bedtime admonitions to me to work after she was asleep and frequently expressed the hope that Mom would not "mess up on her book." Larry was a wise sounding board as the project took twists and turns.

1 The Problem

FOR CENTURIES, WOMEN IN CHINA PRACTICED FOOTBINDING. Footbinding involved folding the foot of a young girl under itself and wrapping it tightly with bandages. The result was that the foot grew to be no more than a few inches long. Women with bound feet were unable to walk normally. They experienced pain and complications, including gangrene, amputation, and even death. Despite these damaging effects, women perpetuated the practice, making sure that their daughters' feet were bound. Footbinding was almost universal among the Chinese and persisted for hundreds of years. Numerous reform efforts failed. Laws against footbinding did nothing to discourage it. Efforts by Western missionaries to inform the Chinese of world opinion about the practice had no effect. But then—in one of the greatest social transformations of the twentieth century—footbinding disappeared in a single generation (Mackie 1996, 2006). Why, given its painful and damaging effects and the efforts to stop it, was the practice of footbinding so widespread and so prolonged? And how, after all the failed efforts, was it finally eliminated?

Modern Western societies typically try to solve social problems using one of three tools: government, with its power to penalize problematic behavior; market incentives, with their ability to motivate productive activity; and education and the internalization of appropriate values. None of these approaches, however, accounts for the demise of footbinding. Laws failed to stop the practice. There is no evidence that markets affected it. And education efforts had little impact. None of the strategies upon which modern societies typically rely explains the persistence and demise of footbinding.

What does? In the late 1800s, British romance novelist Mrs. Archibald Little moved with her new husband to China. More than other British wives, she sought to understand the people around her (Croll 1990; Little 1899). Little became very concerned about the practice of footbinding. She traveled through China studying the practice and the attempts to end it. At one point in her travels, she came across a small community in which the residents had pledged not to bind their daughters' feet and had promised that their sons would marry natural-footed women. Consistent with that pledge, the residents did not practice footbinding. Little recognized the significance of what the community had accomplished. Its example stimulated the creation of Anti-Footbinding Societies in which members made the same promise (Mackie 2006). These societies led to the end of footbinding. They worked because they greatly reduced the negative social consequences of unbound feet. Those earlier social pressures had been strong. Girls whose feet were not bound risked remaining single. But once Anti-Footbinding Societies existed, mothers no longer needed to fear for the futures of daughters with unbound feet. Norms mandating footbinding dissolved. The practice disappeared.

This success story points to a potential source of solutions for intractable social challenges. The failure of governments and markets to solve a number of serious contemporary problems highlights a need for additional tools. Mrs. Little stumbled across a solution implemented by Chinese villagers—a solution that recognized the power of social norms. Norms may also be useful for addressing problems here and now. However, to proactively take advantage of them, we must understand them.

A challenge for anyone trying to understand norms is to determine exactly what they are. Whereas the concept is one of the most widely used in the social sciences, there is little consensus about what norms are and how they emerge. Scholars disagree about the essential elements that constitute a norm. To complicate matters, a variety of other concepts—custom, role, institution, law, value, moral, behavioral regularity, and so forth—are similar to or overlap in significant ways with norms.

I rely on a definition that incorporates elements that many (though not all) scholars view as essential. I define norms as rules, about which there is some degree of consensus, that are socially enforced. Norms may have an internal component. That is, they may define individuals' values and worldviews. They may also be related to patterns of behavior. But while they may overlap with internalized values and behavioral regularities, those features are not unique to norms. Instead, I take the position that social sanctions distinguish norms from other related concepts. Sanctions are an essential element of norms. This does not mean that sanctions are the only things that need an explanation if we want to understand norms, but they are an essential thing to explain. If we cannot explain norm enforcement, then we will not understand norms.

In this book, therefore, I focus on explaining social sanctions. Even narrowing the problem to enforcement (rather than norms in their totality) leaves a range of complicated issues. I do not claim to address them all. Rather, I isolate a small number of key causal factors and mechanisms that are not well understood. Specifically, I link a characteristic of social relations (the interdependence of individuals) to sanctioning. The resulting relational theory of norm enforcement sheds light on a number of theoretical puzzles:

- If a behavior is wrong or harmful, why is it sometimes punished and sometimes not?
- Why do people enforce norms that benefit others rather than themselves?
- Why do we see groups enforce norms far more than makes sense—so much so that they actually harm the group?

- Why do people punish nonconsequential behavior—behavior that has only trivial, if any, effects?

- Why do people sometimes sanction atypical behavior and at other times do nothing?

Theoretical Perspectives on Norms

My approach to understanding norm enforcement builds on and complements existing research. Dominant approaches to thinking about norms focus on the characteristics of the normative act. Each emphasizes a different feature of behavior as important—its consequences for community members, the meaning attached to it, or its frequency. These approaches vary in the extent to which they explicitly address the enforcement problem, and none provides a complete explanation. Nonetheless, each suggests insights that have implications for understanding sanctioning.

The Consequentialist Approach

Behavior consequences approaches hold that norms emerge in response to problematic actions. Early functionalist explanations tended simply to assume the emergence of welfare-enhancing norms. More recent interest-based approaches seek to explain how instrumental individuals manage to produce them.

The standard instrumental argument is that when an individual does something, his behavior does not necessarily affect only him. It may also affect the people around him. Those behavior consequences create a demand for norms (Coleman 1990; see also Demsetz 1967). People who are affected by the behavior would like it to be controlled; they have an interest in regulating it (Heckathorn 1988, 1989). That interest leads them to react negatively to harmful behavior or positively to cooperative actions. Everyone benefits from such sanctioning.

Antismoking norms provide evidence of this dynamic (Ellickson 2001). Americans used to think that smoking was acceptable, even cool. Famed CBS news anchor Edward R. Murrow was shown smoking during his broadcasts. Movie stars smoked on screen. But, eventually, people began hearing about studies showing that secondhand smoke caused lung damage. Smoking was not just the smoker's business anymore. People began reacting negatively to it. Now we hear much more criticism than defense of smoking—because we recognize the dangers.

Smoking is a specific behavior that hurts bystanders. A more general category of behavior that affects others is free-riding. Free-riding occurs in social dilemma situations—those in which the interests of individuals are at odds with those of the group. Such dilemmas are common in social life. For example, any individual might prefer not to make the effort to go to the polls on a cold, rainy night, but if everyone stays home to eat dinner, voter turnout is low and democracy is diminished. Norms researchers identify such social dilemmas in the field, or design studies that create them, and then observe the norms that emerge. They find that, as expected, people punish free-riders (see, for example, Fehr and Gächter 2002; Yamagishi 1986, 1988). Individual pursuit of self-interest in social dilemma situations is theoretically analogous to many specific, concrete behaviors.[1] Just as people react negatively to free-riding and smoking, they will react to other behaviors that have consequences for them.

This argument suggests that as the consequences of a behavior become larger, people's interest in regulating it becomes stronger. They will be more concerned about stopping murder than minor theft. They will be more worried about teenagers getting drunk and driving than about moderate social drinking around the dinner table. We would, therefore, expect stronger punishments to be directed against more damaging behavior (Yamagishi 1988). The benefits of punishing deviance (including the cessation of the harmful act) motivate people to sanction. The larger those potential benefits are relative to the costs, the more sanctioning occurs (Ostrom 1990).

There is a caveat to this argument, however. Rational individuals would presumably prefer to benefit from reductions in harmful behavior without having to make the effort to sanction themselves. They would prefer to avoid the costs—possible retaliation, time, energy, and so forth. They are tempted to free-ride on others' sanctioning efforts. They hope that someone else will ask the smoker at the next table to stop. They hope that someone else will confront the person who cut into line. They hope that someone else will do something about the sugary snacks handed out at their child's day-care center. Because norm enforcement is costly to the individual, but provides benefits to many, it is problematic.

To explain why people punish despite the temptation to do nothing, some researchers have turned to psychological traits. They have found evidence that many people have an innate tendency to react negatively to free-riding (Fehr and Gintis 2007; Gintis et al. 2005). Laboratory experiments have shown that people get angry. Their anger can motivate them to punish despite the costs (Fehr and Gächter 2002). Further, people actually feel good when they punish (Knutson 2004).

Psychological traits differ across individuals and can produce variation in sanctioning. For example, people who do not trust others will support sanctioning systems more than those who do (Yamagishi 1986). Some individuals are more inclined to cooperate than others—cooperating if they expect that others will reciprocate and sanctioning antisocial behavior (Fehr and Gintis 2007).[2]

Whatever the psychological trait of interest in a particular study, in general, approaches that focus on the consequences of behavior suggest that the damaging nature of an action triggers reactions to it.[3] The implication of this view is that norms encourage individuals to cooperate rather than pursue their own self-interest at the expense of the group.[4] Norms enhance group welfare.

But such a view is inconsistent with reality. Norms do not always benefit the group. Sometimes they regulate behaviors that appear to have no consequences at all (fashion in men's ties, for example, or the color of their belts and shoes). And sometimes norms mandate harmful behavior rather than discourage it, as in the case of footbinding.

The Meanings Approach

In part for this reason, many argue that a focus on the consequences of behavior alone is inadequate. One must also examine the meaning of a behavior (see, for example, Fine 2001). These scholars point to instances in which actors do things that make no sense if we consider only the objective outcomes—situations in which consequences alone do not fully explain behavior. Footbinding is only one such destructive practice. Norms of revenge (Elster 1990), rate-busting by workers (Elster 1989), and downward-leveling norms in some ethnic and socioeconomic groups (Portes 1998; Willis 1981) are other examples. It is not only individuals who appear to ignore outcomes—businesses and governments do as well. Countries, for example, may create educational systems that are out of sync with the work lives of their citizens, requiring agricultural workers to study fractions or rural villagers to learn about chemical reactions (Meyer et al. 1997; Meyer, Ramirez, and Soysal 1992).

Pointing to such examples, meanings scholars argue that our explanations will be improved if we consider not only a "logic of consequences" but also a "logic of appropriateness" (March and Olsen 1998; Risse 2000). In addition to (or instead of) weighing the possible costs and benefits of an action, people consider whether it is the right thing to do. Shared meanings become part of how they see the world and, in turn, affect their behavior. On this view, Chinese mothers had their daughters' feet bound because they felt that such behavior was appropriate. Footbinding was taken for granted; it was something that good Chinese families did. Once the practice was established, people had a hard time imagining anything different.

The Creation of Shared Meaning   Scholars seek to explain how these shared meanings emerge. They argue that human beings are active participants in creating their world (Berger and Luckmann 1967). People interact and negotiate to produce views of behavior. They may rely on understandings drawn from previous experience (Dobbin 1994; Rydgren 2007). They may engage in discussions in which they try to determine the "right thing" (Risse 2000). They may negotiate conflicts of interest (Fine 2001) and conflicts over meaning (Graham 2003). They may try to justify choices in a world of conflicting norms (Fine 2001).

Many scholars pay attention to these interaction and negotiation processes. Research suggests that children learn the meaning of friendship in the course of interacting with playmates (Davies 1982; Rizzo 1989, 105), and adolescents develop interpretations of events and establish routines unique to their group (Everhart 1983; Fine 1987; Willis 1981). Researchers interested in social movements describe framing processes and the negotiation of common identities (Cohen 1985, 707; Hunt, Benford, and Snow 1994; Johnston, Larana, and Gusfield 1994; McAdam, McCarthy, and Zald 1996, 6). Political scientists study the construction of norms against torture and other human rights abuses in the international arena (Finnemore 1996a, 1996b; Hawkins 2004). Across a range of substantive issues, interaction and negotiation are widely seen as important for explaining the development of shared meaning.

Shared Meaning Affects Behavior   These shared meanings in turn are thought to affect behavior. Empirical studies seek to provide evidence of such effects.

For example, in the international arena, substantial amounts of research demonstrate that countries that are integrated into the world system are more likely to behave like other countries than those that are isolated. The assumption is that integrated nations have notions of what is appropriate that are consistent with world norms, and they behave accordingly. For example, such research finds that national welfare systems result from countries' involvement in intergovernmental organizations (Thomas and Lauderdale 1988). Purchases of military weapons reflect the meanings associated with particular military hardware and do not necessarily serve national security needs (Eyre and Suchman 1996). Public education programs grow from the symbolic meaning of state-provided education and not so much from the needs of individuals and businesses (Meyer, Ramirez, and Soysal 1992). Such findings are taken as evidence that particular practices or ideologies are taken for granted—part of the cognitive frame through which actors see the world. This meaning, in turn, drives behavior.

The mechanisms at work are not completely clear, however (for a relevant discussion, see Scott 1995). Some formulations of the meanings approach explicitly frame it in opposition to consequentialist theories.

On this view, people do not rationally weigh the costs and benefits of their behavior. Rather, they internalize meanings and identities. Their sense of their identity and what is appropriate affects what they do (see, for example, March and Olsen 1998, 951).

Not all meanings scholars reject rational calculations outright. Some see both consequences and meaning as relevant. Many models are additive, showing that after taking consequences into account, meaning improves predictions (Schneiberg 2007). And some appear to acknowledge a role for external sanctions—again suggesting that interests matter. For example, Meyer and Rowan (1977) argue that the taken-for-granted nature of certain rules provides organizations with legitimacy that protects them from sanctions. That legitimacy may be necessary for an organization to survive (Schneiberg and Clemens 2006). Such views imply that actors consider the results of their decisions and that they prefer to avoid negative reactions. Even more explicitly, Powell (1991, 183) criticizes the tendency to present instrumentalist and meanings approaches in competition with each other. And DiMaggio and Powell (1983) point to coercion and external pressures as mechanisms through which legitimate practices are adopted by specific organizations. Thus, among those who favor meanings approaches, there is ambiguity about the extent to which meaning operates internally (constituting the identity of the actor) or in conjunction with social pressure. To the extent that social pressure operates, the reasons for such pressure (or lack thereof) are often left unexplored.

The Typicality Approach

In practice, empirical work demonstrating the effect of meaning on behavior often finds evidence that actors tend to conform with the majority. This emphasis on conformity in the meanings literature is also found in the third major stream of norms research—the typicality approach. This approach suggests that existing patterns of behavior create normative pressures. In response to these pressures, individuals mimic others. On this view, why did Chinese mothers have their daughters' feet bound? Because that was what everyone else was doing.

Social psychologists have long studied the tendency of individuals to adjust their own behavior to be consistent with that of others'. Sherif's (1936) classic study examined this phenomenon. He shone a light on a screen and asked subjects to evaluate how much the light moved. In reality, it did not move at all. Any apparent shift was merely an optical illusion. Sherif found that estimates that individuals gave when they were part of a group were very similar, while those that isolated actors gave (without knowledge of others' judgments) were more diverse.

Later, Asch's (1951) experiments provided evidence that people would mimic others' choices, not only under conditions of uncertainty (as in Sherif's light studies), but also when those choices were clearly wrong. He showed subjects a set of three lines and asked them to match a fourth line to the one in the group of three that was closest in length. Before subjects made their decisions, however, seven other ostensible participants (confederates of the experimenter) made their choices. Asch found that when all the confederates chose the wrong line, subjects were more likely to choose the wrong line as well.

Contemporary psychological work looks at "descriptive norms." Descriptive norms refer to what people do. They are existing patterns of behavior (Cialdini, Kallgren, and Reno 1991). This research identifies conditions under which information about typical behavior in a particular setting affects an individual's choices. It shows, for example, that hotel guests are more likely to reuse their towels (thereby saving water) if they think that the majority of other guests do so. Visitors to a national park are more likely to steal petrified wood if they think that everyone else does (Cialdini 2007). Scholars explore related phenomena when they seek to understand herd behavior and bandwagons.

A popular intervention on college campuses—the "social norms" approach—similarly relies on the insight that people tend to follow the majority. Proponents argue that students drink too much and engage in other problematic behaviors because they misperceive the social norms on campus (Prentice and Miller 1993). The intervention strategy is to provide students with more accurate information—for example, about how much their peers really do drink. If students realize that others actually drink less than they thought, then they will change their behavior and drink less themselves. A number of campuses have tried this strategy with some success (see, for example, Frauenfelder 2001; Johannessen et al. 1999).

Substantial amounts of research demonstrate a human tendency to conform. But it also shows that the frequency of a behavior affects people through a variety of non-normative mechanisms. For example, individuals may have a taste for conformity (Jones 1984). They may think they will be at a competitive disadvantage if they do not do what others do (Abrahamson and Rosenkopf 1993). They may rely on patterns of behavior as a source of information about strategies that are likely to be successful (Banerjee 1992; Cialdini and Trost 1998; Gale 1996). Or the frequency of a behavior may actually change its value (Katz and Shapiro 1985). If an individual is the only person with a particular credit card, the value of the card will be low because there is no place to use it. But if many people have the same card, then businesses will do what they need to do to accept payment. The card will be widely useable and hence more valuable (Chwe 2001). All of these non-normative mechanisms help to account for individual conformity.

Further, there is little evidence that atypical behavior actually produces negative reactions. The tendency of an individual to conform with the majority is more pronounced when his behavior is public—suggesting that people anticipate social reactions (Deutsch and Gerard 1955). It is not clear that such reactions are actually forthcoming, however. A few scholars have argued that typical behavior triggers mechanisms that lead to punishment of deviations (Opp 1982; Ullmann-Margalit 1977; see also Bicchieri 2006), but there is little empirical work on the issue. Whereas there is substantial research on the tendency of actors to conform with the majority, there is much less work on the conditions under which atypical behavior is sanctioned (Hechter and Opp 2001, 401).

A Relational Theory of Norm Enforcement

The three dominant approaches vary in the extent to which they focus on norm enforcement. Consequentialist research is the most explicit in addressing the enforcement problem. But a focus on the consequences of behavior fails to explain much of the punishment we observe. For meanings scholars, sanctions may be unnecessary if people have internalized a sense of what is appropriate. To the extent that sanctioning is seen as an influence, it is usually not explained. Typicality approaches identify a number of mechanisms through which patterns of behavior affect individuals. Behavioral regularities may create pressures to conform. But the conditions under which those regularities produce sanctioning is unclear.

Despite the differences between them, these dominant perspectives on norms are similar in their emphasis on the characteristics of the regulated *behavior*—its consequences, its meaning, or its frequency. Debates between proponents of these approaches tend to focus on differences in assumptions about actors—most notably, whether they are instrumental or meaning-oriented (see, for example, Gintis et al. 2005; Ostrom, Gardner, and Walker 1994; Risse 2000). The characteristics of behavior in conjunction with (more or less rational) actors affect outcomes.

In this book, I accept that the characteristics of behavior identified by these approaches are important for understanding norms. I shift my focus to the characteristics of social relations. I build on insights from existing research to develop a theory that explains how a specific characteristic of social relations affects norm enforcement.

People enforce norms when they sanction—when they treat someone who engages in a particular behavior differently from those who do not. We might, for example, glare or yell at someone who cuts into line but say nothing to the others standing there. We might treat someone who sleeps with her best friend's boyfriend worse than someone who respects boundaries. We might give children time-outs for hitting others and hugs for behaving well. Informal sanctions are relative—treating people better or worse depending on how they behave.

As the consequentialist approach highlights, it is not at all obvious why people enforce norms. Indeed, there is good reason to expect them not to do so. Such sanctioning efforts may be time-consuming, emotionally draining, and potentially embarrassing. A mother may be too tired to deal with her child running around the swimming pool deck; a coworker might not want to muster the energy it takes to confront a colleague about bad behavior. Sanctioners also run the risk of retaliation—anything from anger to ridicule to the end of a relationship to physical injury. An inner-city resident may reasonably be afraid to confront the drug dealers hanging out on the corner. Why, then, do people punish?

In some situations, sanctioning is essentially costless (Pettit 1993). For example, it happens as a side effect of something we were going to do anyway for another reason. Or, it occurs as people give respect or status to others (Brennan and Pettit 2004; McAdams 1997; but see Kitts 2006). Sometimes preventing ourselves from sanctioning takes effort. It may take self-control for us not to lose our temper at a particularly egregious action or at the child whose misbehavior has occurred one too many times. And sometimes sanctioning simply involves avoiding someone whose behavior suggests that he is unreliable.

But, much of the time, sanctioning is costly. It is uncomfortable to ask someone at a neighboring table not to smoke. It is physically dangerous to confront people engaged in criminal and violent behavior. Often it is easier just to let things slide—and hope that someone else takes care of the issue.

The problem inherent in sanctioning is illustrated by one of Aesop's fables, "The Mice in Council" (Coleman 1990, 270–71). The mice lived a very good life in a home with plenty of food. Their one problem was the cat who would eat the mice when they ventured out of their holes. The mice got together to decide what to do. They all agreed that the best solution was to put a bell around the cat's neck so that they would be able to hear the cat approaching in time to get to safety. All the mice enthusiastically applauded this suggestion until one wise old mouse asked, "Who is going to put the bell around the cat's neck?"

There were very large costs associated with attaching the bell to the cat—the altruistic martyr might be eaten. Similarly, there can be large costs associated with sanctioning. Given the costs, it is easier to do nothing—to hope that someone else addresses the problem, to hope that someone else will put the bell on the cat. Of course, if everyone does this, then sanctioning does not occur and norms are weak or nonexistent. We know, however, that people *do* sanction. We see it all around us and adjust our own behavior in anticipation. Why do people sanction in the face of costs?

I argue that social relations are a key factor. A long history of research points to the importance of social relations for a range of outcomes. As early as the 1300s, Arab scholar Ibn Kaldhun emphasized the role of cohesion in tribal societies (Gellner 1988). Centuries later, in the 1830s, Alexis de Tocqueville ([1835, 1840] 2000) expressed his fascination with groups and the contribution of voluntary associations to democracy. Soon after, sociologist Emile Durkheim (1951) pointed to the importance of social integration in the most personal of decisions, suicide.

Social capital research similarly emphasizes the importance of relationships. While definitions vary, social capital is generally thought to be "connections among individuals—social networks and the norms of reciprocity . . . that arise from them" (Putnam 2000, 19).[5] Networks are thought to be associated with strong norms—norms that encourage individuals to do things for others, even if those others cannot return the favor. These networks and norms are credited with producing a range of effects, including improved market performance and effective government (Putnam 1993).

This focus on social relations is also found in other contemporary research. The meanings approach to norms, for example, suggests that meanings are developed and have consequences in communities (see, for example, Guler, Guillén, and MacPherson 2002). Meanings are relevant in the context of relationships.

Similarly, social controls are imposed through groups and networks. Theoretical work suggests that members' dependence on a group affects the demands that the group can make of them (Hechter 1987). Social psychologists report evidence that cohesive groups are better able to restrain their members than noncohesive groups (Homans 1950; but see Flache 1996; and Flache and Macy 1996). Criminologists highlight the importance of community cohesion for controlling criminal and delinquent behavior (Bursik and Grasmick 1993; Sampson, Raudenbush, and Earls 1997). Legal scholars describe how tight-knit groups as diverse as New York diamond dealers, midwestern businessmen, and California cattle ranchers are able to resolve conflicts without turning to the law (Bernstein 1992; Ellickson 1991; Macauley 1963). Other legal work highlights the role of reciprocal relationships in sanctioning (see, for example, McAdams 1997; Posner 1996a).

This long and varied research tradition provides good reason to believe that social relations are important for a variety of outcomes—including norm enforcement. Yet norms researchers do not always pay attention to them explicitly. Further, the reasons for a connection between "groupness" and sanctioning are not well understood. Research suggests that social relations matter for norm enforcement, but it leaves unresolved many questions regarding how and why.

In this book I provide one answer. I assume that people care about what others think of them. This concern affects not only their behavior but also their sanctioning activity. When individuals make decisions about whether or not to punish someone, they consider the likely reactions of people around them.

If people care about how others treat them, then the structure of their relations matters. Not all relationships are equally influential. When people value their ties with others, they are dependent on those others. They are concerned with maintaining valued relationships and in provoking positive (rather than negative) reactions. This concern affects their enforcement decisions. Accordingly, variation in the strength of relationships—that is, variation in the social structure in which people are embedded—produces changes in sanctioning. In particular, interdependence increases norm enforcement.

In addition, if people care about how others treat them, then they will prefer to enforce norms that they think others want. But they have a problem. Their problem is determining just what behaviors others would like to see punished. Sometimes, the answer is easy. Acceptable practices are codified in laws and organizational rules. Groups come together to explicitly discuss and agree on appropriate behavior. Often, however, there is no formal mechanism and people have to figure out things on their own. In order to do so, they need to look for clues as to what kinds of sanctioning people will approve. An important source of such clues is the characteristics of behavior—its consequences, meaning, and frequency. These characteristics provide the individual with indicators of the behaviors that people approve or disapprove, and in turn, the sanctioning efforts to which they will respond positively.

In sum, only part of norm enforcement is explained by the characteristics of behavior. Those characteristics provide information about the actions that people would like to see sanctioned. They provide clues regarding the sanctions people are likely to approve—thereby determining *what* gets sanctioned. The characteristics of social relations provide incentives that give people a reason to sanction—helping to account for *why* they do so.[6] This book explains these dynamics, laying out a relational theory of norm enforcement.

Using Laboratory Experiments to Study Norms

In addition to presenting the theory, the book describes the empirical support. To test my theoretical ideas, I developed three standardized experimental settings—the Norms Game, the Metanorms Game, and the Expectations Game. I conducted a series of laboratory experiments in these settings. Taken together, the experimental results point to the importance of social relations for norm enforcement.

Experimental methods are a useful tool for testing the theory. Norms are difficult to study in naturally occurring settings. Even the essential task of identifying a norm can be a challenge. It is particularly hard to measure sanctioning. In surveys, people do not always accurately report their treatment of others or others' treatment of them. And researchers who try to observe sanctions are not able to be in all places at all times and therefore cannot get a complete picture. In addition to measurement challenges, researchers often face difficulties in disentangling causal relations. For example, do norms cause behavior? Do patterns of behavior lead to norm enforcement? Or both?

Lab experiments can help to address both challenges. Researchers can create manipulations that are consistent with the theoretical causal factors, and they can create settings in which outcome behaviors can easily be observed.

Further, because experiments involve random assignment to treatment conditions, inferences of causal order are more straightforward than when relying on other kinds of data. Random assignment is a strength of experimental methods—and a great help in disentangling causal relations in the context of norm enforcement.

I am interested in developing a theoretical understanding of norms that can then be applied to a variety of substantive settings. I seek to identify simple social structural features, the mechanisms they trigger, and the resulting norms. At this stage, I neither need nor want all of the complexity of the naturally occurring world. Laboratory experiments are perfect for my purposes.

Artificiality

Some researchers question the utility of experimental methods. They argue that lab experiments have low external validity. They wonder how an experiment conducted in an artificial situation can tell us anything about social processes in everyday life. Such criticisms raise the question of whether, despite their value for testing causal theories, lab experiments can tell us anything useful about norms.

Zelditch (1969) provides the beginnings of an answer to this question. He wrote a piece entitled "Can You Really Study an Army in the Laboratory?" Many of us would quickly respond no—one can not replicate in the lab relationships between troops, the strains of the battlefield, or anything else that matters.

Zelditch argues otherwise. He admits that the lab is nothing like the real world. "If the idea is that the laboratory group resembles the smaller kinds of groups found in natural settings, then the idea is wrong. . . . [T]he laboratory group is not like any concrete setting in society" (Zelditch 1969, 528–29). We cannot create anything that looks and feels like a battlefield in the lab. In fact, to try to do so would be misguided. An experimental setting that mimics naturally occurring situations provides little advantage. The purpose of the lab is not to recreate reality—with all of the attendant challenges of measurement and disentangling causal relations and mechanisms. Instead it is to "create certain theoretically relevant aspects of social situations under controlled conditions" (Zelditch 1969, 530).

In other words, once we have a theory, we develop a setting appropriate for testing that theory—one that excludes the confounding factors that might exist in naturally occurring situations. If the theory is supported, then we have greater confidence in it.

We should then apply it across a range of settings (Willer and Walker 2007). If a theory is supported both in the lab and in the field, then we have confidence not only in the theory but also in its usefulness for explaining real-world phenomena. If it is supported in lab, but not in the field, that suggests that additional, unidentified factors are interacting with the theoretical causal factors.[7] Such potential interactions can and should be explored further. This process will lead to theoretical development. A combination of lab experiments and field studies can effectively help us develop useful theoretical knowledge.

College Students as Subjects

What about reliance on college students as subjects? One of the frequent objections to lab experiments is that college students may behave differently from other people. If so, how can relying on them be justified?

A key issue is whether the characteristics of the student participants interact in a systematic way with the causal factors of interest. Is there any reason to think, for example, that the relation between the harm caused by a behavior and reactions to that behavior would be different for college students than for community members in general (controlling for all other factors)? The consequentialist approach suggests that people will react more negatively to bigger losses. Suppose that college students really are different from others—imagine that they think less about the long term. Even if this is the case, they would presumably still dislike losing a thousand dollars more than ten dollars. Their shortsightedness might lead them to have a generally lower tendency to sanction, but one would still expect them to react more negatively to the larger loss. Only if subject characteristics interact with the theoretical causal factors (for example, students' short-sightedness led them to be more upset if they lost ten dollars than a thousand dollars), would we expect to see different results for college students than for others.

In other words, if college students are different from the general population, but those differences do not interact with the theoretical factors of interest, then we might well see higher or lower levels of overall norm enforcement with college students than with other populations. But the experimental manipulations would produce effects regardless of the subjects involved.

When I began my research on norms, I did not have any a priori reason to expect differences that might interact with the theoretical factors in which I was interested. Existing relevant research suggested little reason to expect non-college student populations to behave differently than students in the lab. Studies of social dilemmas in India, rural Colombia, and the Italian Alps, for example, have produced the same findings as those using American college students (Ostrom 2005, 93–97).[8]

Further, given the lack of information about differences across potential subgroups, it would be difficult to identify a superior subject pool. As a practical matter, it can be prohibitively expensive to do experiments with a national (or international) random sample. Researchers are generally, therefore, forced to choose a particular subject pool. Any nonrandomly selected pool would raise the same issue as college students. None would be representative of the general population. For all of these reasons, I relied on student participants, recognizing that future applied work may lead to modifications of the theory for different populations.

The Plan of the Book

This book presents a new relational theory of norm enforcement and describes its empirical support. The theory identifies a particular characteristic of social relations—interdependence—and articulates key mechanisms linking it with norm enforcement.

Chapters 2 through 5 describe the basic research. They develop the theoretical argument and discuss the experimental results. Each chapter begins with an illustration that raises a theoretical question. I then present the theory, describe the experiments in broad strokes, summarize the findings, and conclude with a discussion. Readers interested in the methodological details can find them in the methods appendix.

In Chapter 6, I reflect on some of the substantive implications of the relational theory of norms. To begin to think about how useful the theory might be for explaining life outside of the lab, I apply the theory to several substantive issues: Why does the permissiveness of norms regulating heterosexual sex vary? How might norms contribute to an understanding of the informal control of crime and delinquency across neighborhoods? Why did nations support the International Criminal Court, making a costly commitment to the enforcement of human rights norms? Lab experiments are very useful for testing causal theories. To evaluate a theory's broader utility, it must be applied outside the lab. In this chapter I describe some beginning explorations.

Chapter 7 argues that norms do not exist in a vacuum. Rather, they operate side by side with government penalties and market incentives. Norms are often overlooked as a source of solutions to social problems, however. Further, policy interventions based on governments or markets may have unintended effects on norms. I discuss one way of thinking about the relation between norms and law and between norms and markets, and describe an experimental test of the predictions regarding the effect of a strong legal system on social relations. I also provide an illustration of how recognizing the power of social norms might affect the way we think about policy, focusing in particular on education.

Chapter 8 concludes the book by summarizing the key findings. I come back to the enforcement puzzles raised at the beginning of this chapter and discuss the solutions suggested by the theory. I describe what the theory tells us and what it leaves out, and I suggest an approach to integrating the diverse literature on norms and enforcement.

The key contribution of the book is that it describes how and why a particular characteristic of social relations affects norm enforcement. My intent is to add to the growing body of theoretical knowledge about norms. My hope is that increased theoretical understanding will have practical payoffs.

2 Social Relations

Controlling Disruptive Colleagues

MANY ACADEMICS HAVE ENCOUNTERED THE ABUSIVE FACulty member—the one who yells at, swears at, threatens, intimidates, and generally undermines colleagues. Such faculty may harass students as well as peers. And they may continue their damaging behaviors for their entire careers without anyone doing anything about it. Such nonaction by colleagues is not surprising. It is understandable that any individual would want to avoid the unpleasant task of confronting bad behavior. No one wants to be the victim of retaliation—increased verbal abuse or bad-mouthing around the university or the discipline. But sometimes colleagues take action against an out-of-control individual. Why? And under what conditions are they likely to do so? More generally, why do people undertake personally costly enforcement efforts in response to harmful behavior? What factors might offset some of the costs?

Theoretical Background and Development

To answer this question, I begin by accepting the consequentialist argument that harmful behaviors (like those of the abusive colleague) provoke negative reactions. I start here, because of the three dominant approaches to norms, consequentialist research is the most explicit in addressing the sanctioning problem. As described in the previous chapter, according to this approach, an individual's actions do not necessarily just affect him. They may also affect people around him. When somebody uses more than his share of irrigation water, other community members cannot water their crops. When somebody steals, victims lose their property. When one person smokes, bystanders breathe the polluted air. When somebody cheats, the dupe suffers.

Those people who are negatively affected have an interest in controlling the behavior (Coleman 1990; Heckathorn 1988, 1989).[1] When sufficiently strong, that interest leads them to punish harmful acts. Individuals who want water for their crops will confront the person who uses too much. Those who own property will support efforts to punish thieves. People who do not like cigarette smoke will react negatively to smokers. The larger the consequences of the behavior (and the related benefits of punishing it), the more severe the punishment is likely to be (Fehr and Gächter 2002; Yamagishi 1988).

The argument suggests that department faculty are more likely to punish bad behavior that is particularly egregious and may lead to bad publicity, reduce resources, or create other substantial costs. They will enforce norms controlling faculty misbehavior when it has significant implications for their welfare.

Interdependence

Given this view of norms as a response to damaging behavior, is there any reason to think that social relations would have an effect on enforcement? To explore this issue, I focus on a particular characteristic of relationships—*interdependence*. Dependence refers to the value that people place on their relationships and the goods that they can gain from them (Emerson 1962, 1972; Molm 1997; Molm and Cook 1995).[2] If we think about all of the things that human beings value in life—love, money, respect, and so forth—many of them require other people. Individuals cannot get these things on their own. The more that they need others to attain things they value, the more dependent they are. And the more mutually dependent people are, the higher the levels of interdependence and cohesion in a group.[3]

Because individuals are dependent on those around them, their well-being is tied, to some extent, to others. People benefit more from their relationships when those with whom they interact have something to offer. They are more likely to get a ride to the store if someone they know has a functioning car. Victims of Hurricane Katrina who had ties to relatives who themselves lacked resources experienced difficulties (Fussell 2008). When Nigerian villagers move to Lagos in hope of a better life, they look for a relative or some other connection who can give them a start. If all the relative can afford to offer is food for a night, that is not much help. The more able the Lagos resident is to provide assistance, the better off the newcomer (Packer 2006).

Interdependence and Norm Enforcement

The insight that people's well-being is affected by the welfare of those with whom they interact is relevant for understanding norms. Antisocial behavior directly harms individuals. The victim of a theft or mugging is hurt. Antisocial behavior also affects the people who interact with the victim. When the offender is caught, the victim is relieved, but so are the victim's friends and family.

In other words, norm enforcement produces two kinds of gains. One gain is the *direct* benefit—a reduction in antisocial behavior. Individuals do not have to fear being raped or mugged. They do not have to worry about being short of irrigation water. They do not have to protect themselves from cheaters.

The other source of gain is the *indirect* benefit that operates through social relations. Norm enforcement produces indirect benefits when it enhances the ability of individuals to interact. Such enhancement occurs when sanctioning produces benefits for everyone—and when those benefits, in turn, facilitate more (profitable) interaction.[4] In other words, people gain when they interact with others who have also benefited from deviance being discouraged. Not only are individuals happy that they were not raped; they further benefit from the fact that their friends were not raped either. Individuals benefit when they are not victimized; they also gain when their neighborhood is safe and secure. People succeed when they have adequate water for growing crops; they are also better off when everyone in the community is able to grow sufficient food. Individuals prosper when they are not cheated; they also profit when levels of cheating are relatively low.

Thus while people may care about their relationships with the deviant and be concerned about potential retaliation, they are also affected by the well-being of all of the others with whom they interact. The more dependent they are, the more their well-being is connected to that of others. Similarly, the increased ability to exchange that can be produced by norm enforcement grows in importance as people become dependent on each other. Interdependence magnifies the benefits of norm enforcement, thereby providing greater incentives to sanction, and in turn, producing stronger norms. The consequences of behavior interact with interdependence to affect norm enforcement.[5]

The behavior consequences explanation predicts that when behavior is harmful, people want to punish it. But incorporating social relations into the theory modifies the prediction. The relational theory of norms suggests that enforcement efforts vary with the interdependence of actors. Sanctions are strongest when behaviors have large negative consequences *and* when group members are highly interdependent. People may be inclined to punish smoking when they are aware of the harmful consequences, but they are even more likely to do so in cohesive groups. Faculty may want to sanction bad behavior when it has serious consequences for the welfare of department members, but their punishments will be more severe when they value their relationships with each other and are dependent on each other for valued goods (professional advice, social support, and so forth). Harmful behavior alone does not predict sanctions. Rather, behavior in conjunction with social relations affects enforcement.

Heterogeneity and Conflicts of Interests

The argument thus far assumes that everyone has the same interests in particular behaviors. In life, however, interests often conflict. Suppose that it is hiring time in an academic department. Reading applications, conducting interviews, and engaging in general recruiting efforts takes time and energy. Departments need faculty to make such efforts. Everyone has an interest in hiring the strongest possible candidate. But individual faculty may disagree about the type of person that ought to be hired. A criminologist, for example, may benefit more from hiring a fellow criminologist. Demographers may prefer another demographer.

Such conflicts are found in a range of settings across a number of dividing lines. In the rural American West, for example, environmentalists work to protect land with wilderness characteristics from degradation. Their work is good for wilderness lovers who like to hike and backpack. But it may not be so good for ranchers who want to graze their cattle. Similarly, ranchers may work to protect their right to graze cattle on public lands. Ranchers benefit from low-cost feed. But hikers and campers resent the muddied streams and cow pies left behind.

Women experience different costs and benefits associated with producing and raising children than do men. Women are also subject to particular kinds of violence that men usually do not need to think about. Most men, for example, do not worry about being raped or sexually assaulted if they walk home alone after dark.

It is relatively straightforward to understand why people might enforce norms that sustain their position (Hechter and Borland 2001). We expect individuals to enforce norms that benefit them. In other words, in situations in which interests conflict, the most likely outcome would seem to be that people will enforce norms that encourage the behaviors they prefer. Faculty will either withdraw to their own research and teaching or work for outcomes consistent with their interests. Environmentalists will either give up or, if they act, they will fight to protect public lands. Ranchers will either do nothing or will work to protect the right to graze cattle. Men will look after themselves or will try to maintain male privileges. Wall Street financial wizards will endeavor to protect their financial interests at the expense of their employees and the public. Assuming that people do something rather than nothing, we would expect their doing something to involve supporting norms that benefit them.

Sometimes, however, people enforce norms that benefit others more than themselves. Sometimes faculty pursue the good of the department as a whole. Sometimes environmentalists work together with ranchers. And sometimes men enforce norms that benefit women. Why do they do this? More generally, why do people enforce benevolent norms and under what conditions are they likely to do so?

The theoretical insight that people gain when those with whom they interact are in better shape can help us to answer this question. A woman who does not have to worry about being raped on her way home from work after dark is better off than one who does. Women therefore have reason to support norms against violence. It is not surprising that women work for women's rights. But the well-being of a woman affects not only her, but potentially her husband, children, and others. While husbands and children do not benefit directly from punishing violence against women, they gain indirectly because of their relationships with their wives or mothers. They are better off because someone on whom they are dependent is safe.

The environmentalist who works with the locals is happier when his local friends are doing well. The rancher gains when his family members can earn extra income by working in a booming local ecotourist economy.

When people are dependent on those who benefit from a particular behavior, they gain when the other is better off and, therefore, have reason to enforce norms encouraging that behavior—even if they themselves would prefer something different. An environmentalist surrounded by like-minded friends might enforce pro-environmental norms. But an environmentalist connected to a community of ranchers might well behave differently. Faculty members will support norms that benefit the department as a whole, rather than just themselves, when they have strong relationships with each other.

The positive interpretation of this dynamic is that people may enforce benevolent norms—norms that directly benefit others. A more negative interpretation is that people can be co-opted. Their dependence on others can lead them to enforce norms that they do not prefer and in which they do not believe. For example, environmentalists may enforce pro-development norms.

In sum, people will tend to punish harmful behavior—the greater the harm, the larger the punishment—but this tendency will be moderated by their dependence relations. Groups with high levels of interdependence will be more punitive. Further, relationships may lead people to enforce a norm even if they would prefer a different norm to be in effect.

The Norms Game

To test these predictions, I developed the Norms Game, a game in which four participants interacted with each other over networked computers for a large number of rounds. Participants had two kinds of choices to make.

First, they could give points to the group project. If an individual gave to the group, all members benefited, but the individual bore a cost. Because everyone gained, they all had an interest in the donation behavior. They had reason to want others to donate while preferring not to incur the expense of doing so themselves. The number of contributions that group members made over the course of the experiment produced a donation rate for the group.

Second, participants were able to exchange points. On each round they could give their points to others. When making decisions about giving points, they could consider whether or not an individual had contributed to the group. The difference between the points given to those who donated and those who did not provided a measure of the sanctions directed at non-contributors.

Experiment 1

I conducted two experiments using the Norms Game framework. In Experiment 1, I looked at whether people impose harsher punishments against behavior that produces greater harm and whether this tendency is enhanced when group members are interdependent. I also looked to see whether the size of the punishment affects donation rates.

To do this, I manipulated two experimental conditions (Table 2.1). I varied the level of interdependence between group members. When interdependence was high, the points that people received from others were worth two times the individual's own points—participants could make more money if they exchanged with others than if they did not. When interdependence was low, points received from others were worth the same as the individual's own points.[6] There was no reason for subjects to interact; they could do just as well alone.

I also varied the consequences of the donation behavior—the benefits that group members received if an individual contributed to the group. In the large consequences condition, all group members received 6 points; in the small consequences condition they received only 2 points. In both conditions, it cost the individual 20 points to make a donation.

TABLE 2.1 Experiment 1 conditions

	Small Behavior Consequences	*Large Behavior Consequences*
Low Interdependence	1:1 2 points	1:1 6 points
High Interdependence	1:2 2 points	1:2 6 points

SOURCE: Based on research published in "Norm Enforcement in Heterogeneous Groups: Sanctioning by Majorities and Isolated Minorities." *Rationality and Society* 20(2): 147–72 (2008).
NOTE: I ran fourteen groups of four in each condition, for a total of fifty-six groups.

The results show that when failure to donate had large consequences (donations produced substantial benefits for group members), the participants imposed more severe punishments than they did when the consequences were small. Increases in behavior consequences led to larger sanctions. But this was only true in groups in which people were highly interdependent (Table 2.2 and Model 1 in Table 2.3). If we return

TABLE 2.2 Mean norm enforcement and donations across interdependence and behavior consequences conditions (experiment 1)

		Small Behavior Consequences		Large Behavior Consequences	
		Mean	SD	Mean	SD
Low Interdependence	Norm Enforcement	1.33	(1.28)	1.75	(.951)
	Donations	.438	(.210)	.731	(.150)
High Interdependence	Norm Enforcement	1.41	(1.38)	5.63[a]	(2.76)
	Donations	.607	(.240)	.884	(.148)

SOURCE: Drawn from "Norm Enforcement in Heterogeneous Groups: Sanctioning by Majorities and Isolated Minorities." *Rationality and Society* 20(2): 147–72 (2008).
NOTE: $N = 14$ in each condition except where noted.
[a]$N = 12$.

TABLE 2.3 OLS regression for the effects of interdependence and behavior consequences on norm enforcement and donations (experiment 1)

	Norm Enforcement		Donations	
	Model 1		Model 2[a]	
Intercept	1.12	(.712)	.336****	(.0701)
Interdependence	−1.81	(1.01)	.125*	(.0596)
Consequences	.105	(.159)	.0345*	(.0160)
Interdependence × Consequences	.949***	(.230)	——	
Norm Enforcement	——		.0370**	(.0117)
R-Square	.53		.43	

SOURCE: Drawn from "Norm Enforcement in Heterogeneous Groups: Sanctioning by Majorities and Isolated Minorities." *Rationality and Society* 20(2): 147–72 (2008).
NOTE: Standard errors are in parentheses.
[a]Last 12 rounds.
$N = 54$.
*$p < .05$, **$p < .01$, ****$p < .001$, ***$p < .0001$ (two-tailed tests)

to the example of the misbehaving professor, these results suggest that the fact that the professor causes a lot of harm will not be sufficient to provoke sanctioning. Rather, colleagues will punish if they have close relationships with each other. Harmful behaviors are more likely to be punished in close-knit departments than elsewhere.

In turn, those punishments are effective. The results show that norm enforcement was correlated with donations (Model 2 in Table 2.3).[7] The more severe the punishment, the more likely people were to contribute.[8] The implication is that when misbehaving faculty are punished, they are less likely to behave badly.

Experiment 2

In Experiment 2, I looked at whether social relations could lead people to enforce norms they do not prefer or fail to enforce norms they like.

TABLE 2.4 Experiment 2 conditions

	Small (Same) Consequences	Large (Different) Consequences
Low Interdependence	1:1 — Majority G = 2 — Minority G = 2	1:1 — Majority G = 6 — Minority P = 6
High Interdependence	1:2 — Majority G = 2 — Minority G = 2	1:2 — Majority G = 6 — Minority P = 6

SOURCE: Based on research published in "Norm Enforcement in Heterogeneous Groups: Sanctioning by Majorities and Isolated Minorities." *Rationality and Society* 20(2): 147–72 (2008).

NOTE: I ran fourteen groups of four in each condition, for a total of fifty-six groups.

To do this, I varied the number of projects and the consequences of dona-tions to each (Table 2.4). When consequences were small, nobody gained much from contributions to the group project. When consequences were large, three of the group members (the "majority") benefited most from donations to Project G.[9] One (the "minority") benefited most from do-nations to Project P.[10] Again, as in Experiment 1, I manipulated the level of interdependence between group members.

I looked to see whether interactions between participants affected the extent to which they enforced pro-G norms. The results show that when majority members interacted with the lone individual, their norm enforcement efforts were weak (Model 1 in Table 2.6; see Table 2.5 for mean sanctions and donations across conditions). Punishments di-

TABLE 2.5 Mean norm enforcement and donations across interdependence and behavior consequences conditions (experiment 2)

		Small (Same) Behavior Consequences		Large (Different) Behavior Consequences	
		Mean	SD	Mean	SD
Low Interdependence	*Majority*				
	Norm Enforcement	1.78	(1.93)	2.01	(1.07)
	Donation to G	.429	(.194)	.681	(.225)
	Minority				
	Norm Enforcement	.250	(3.55)	.153	(1.20)
	Donation to G	.351	(.376)	.149	(.174)
	Group				
	Norm Enforcement	1.92	(1.69)	1.44	(.713)
High Interdependence	*Majority*				
	Norm Enforcement	1.97	(1.93)	2.87	(3.17)
	Donation to G	.468	(.314)	.720	(.218)
	Minority				
	Norm Enforcement	1.18	(2.89)	3.26[a]	(5.38)
	Donation to G	.524	(.331)	.304	(.271)
	Group				
	Norm Enforcement	1.74	(1.48)	2.67	(2.35)

SOURCE: Drawn from "Norm Enforcement in Heterogeneous Groups: Sanctioning by Majorities and Isolated Minorities." *Rationality and Society* 20(2): 147–72 (2008).
NOTE: $N=14$ in each condition except where noted.
[a] $N=12$.

TABLE 2.6 OLS regression explaining pro-G norm enforcement (experiment 2)

	Majority Enforcement Model 1[a]		Minority Enforcement Model 2[b]	
Intercept	1.72	(.963)	3.68*	(1.48)
Interdependence	.779	(1.45)	−3.54	(2.10)
Consequences	.0999	(.376)	−1.18	(.660)
Interdependence × Consequences	.184	(.519)	2.21*	(.952)
Majority Points to Each Other	.376**	(.138)	——	
Minority Points to Majority	−.429**	(.124)	——	
R-Square	.26		.11	

SOURCE: Drawn from "Norm Enforcement in Heterogeneous Groups: Sanctioning by Majorities and Isolated Minorities." *Rationality and Society* 20(2): 147–72 (2008).
NOTE: Standard errors are in parentheses.
[a]$N=56$.
[b]$N=54$.
*p<.05, **p<.01 (two-tailed tests)

rected at failures to contribute to Project G declined. As they interacted with each other, however, their sanctions became larger (Model 1 in Table 2.6). Their sanctioning efforts were affected by their interactions.

The minority individual in each group also made different sanctioning decisions depending on his interactions. The more that minorities exchanged with majority members, the more they enforced the pro-G norm the majority members preferred (Model 2 in Table 2.6).[11] These results show that interaction patterns did indeed affect enforcement.

In turn, group norm enforcement increased the likelihood that majority members contributed to G (Model 1 in Table 2.7). The stronger the sanctions, the more they complied with the pro-G norm.

But group enforcement did not affect donations by minorities (Model 2 in Table 2.7). It appears that the norm simply was not strong enough to motivate them to donate to G, given that they preferred P. Ironically, the three majority members followed the pro-G norm but did not enforce it. Simultaneously, minority individuals enforced the norm but did not follow it.

The results of the two experiments show that behavior consequences alone were not sufficient to predict sanctioning. Instead, punishments

TABLE 2.7 OLS regression explaining donations to project G (experiment 2)

| | Majority Donations | | Minority Donations | |
	Model 1		Model 2	
Intercept	1.79*	(.0675)	.420****	(.102)
Interdependence	−.00483	(.0525)	.149	(.0794)
Consequences	.116****	(.0260)	−.109**	(.0393)
Group Norm Enforcement	.0850****	(.0158)	.0283	(.0239)
R-Square	.51		.20	

SOURCE: Drawn from "Norm Enforcement in Heterogeneous Groups: Sanctioning by Majorities and Isolated Minorities." *Rationality and Society* 20(2): 147–72 (2008).
NOTE: Standard errors are in parentheses.
$N = 56$.
*$p < .05$, **$p < .01$, ***$p < .001$, ****$p < .0001$ (two-tailed tests)

were strongest when the consequences of donating were large and when people were highly interdependent. In groups in which people were affected differently by donation decisions, interactions discouraged people from enforcing norms they wanted (as was the case for the three majority members) and encouraged them to enforce norms they did not prefer (as was the case for the lone individual).

Benevolent Norms

The argument made in this chapter suggests that social relations, not just behavior consequences, affect enforcement. Social relations can enhance the benefits of sanctioning. This mechanism encourages enforcement generally; it can also lead people to enforce benevolent norms. Consider, for example, Richard Felson's (2000) claim that there is a norm of chivalry—a norm that says that women should be protected from violence. His suggestion raises the question of why men would enforce such a norm. According to the consequentialist argument, people punish behavior when it affects them. If it does not, they have no reason to react. On this view, men might well enforce norms of male dominance.[12] It is much less obvious why they would enforce norms protecting women.

The argument in this chapter suggests a partial explanation. Men do not necessarily enforce such norms because they carry some internalized sense of chivalry or fairness (though that may be part of it). Rather, they do so because they have social connections to women. Men often depend on women for things they want and need. They therefore gain when the women in their lives are better off. In turn, they have reason to support norms that benefit women.

Scholars describe similar dynamics in other settings. For example, while norms supporting discrimination and segregation in the American South produced a perceived benefit for white southerners, they also limited opportunities for exchange in business settings. Business leaders therefore had an interest in desegregation (Rosenberg 1991).

An implication of the argument is that benevolent punishments are most likely to be triggered if people recognize that they are dependent on others and that others' well-being affects them. If they do not see their own dependence, they have little reason to enforce benevolent norms.

Discussion

Why do some academic departments have more antisocial behavior than others? It is not just (or even at all) because particularly nasty people work in them. It is also because of the structure of ties between department members—the extent to which they value their relationships with each other. Interdependence relations (not just the obvious interests of individuals in particular outcomes) affect faculty support for various department goals and the ability of a department to move forward collectively.

The mechanism described in this chapter explains one way in which social relations affect the gains associated with sanctioning, and in turn, actual enforcement efforts. Relationships magnify the benefits of sanctioning, increasing the size of benefits relative to the costs. In turn, these increased benefits strengthen incentives to sanction, leading to more norm enforcement.

This explanation sheds light on why the same behavior might be treated differently in different social contexts.[13] Harmful behavior may or may not be punished, depending on the relationships between group members.

The findings complement recent consequentialist research that explores how individual internal states lead people to punish harmful behavior. That work suggests that while some people are self-interested, others are inclined to cooperate. They want to cooperate (at least if others are doing so), and they punish those who do not (Fehr and Gächter 2002).[14] The results in this chapter suggest that whatever those innate tendencies, individuals' actual sanctioning efforts vary with the strength of their relations with other group members. Groups in which people are interdependent will be more punitive than those in which individuals do not need each other. Social relations can lead people to enforce norms they do not prefer or fail to enforce norms they would actually like to be in effect.

But why do people sanction rather than simply free-ride on others' efforts? Prosocial individuals may be motivated to punish bad behavior because it makes them angry (Fehr and Gächter 2002). Emotions do not necessarily eliminate concerns with costs and benefits, however. And even if enforcement and social relations together produce large benefits, individuals would still presumably prefer to get those benefits without having to bear the costs of sanctioning. That is, they would prefer to free-ride, to wait for others to take action.

Further, why do people sanction when the obvious personal benefits are smaller than their costs? What if even the indirect benefits are not sufficient to offset the costs that individuals incur when they punish deviance?

Something else must be going on. In the next chapter, I suggest one possibility, describing a second mechanism linking social relations to norm enforcement.

3 Metanorms

Even Tyrants Care What Others Think

IN 1988, CHILEAN DICTATOR AUGUSTO PINOCHET SIGNED ONTO the International Convention against Torture. That same year, the United States also became a signatory. By acceding to this treaty, American and Chilean officials (as well as the 128 other signatories) gave foreign countries the right to prosecute them should they engage in torture. In essence, they made a costly commitment to the enforcement of a particular human rights norm. Ten years later, consistent with the terms of the anti-torture convention, Pinochet was arrested by British police and charged by a Spanish prosecutor. The sanctioning mechanism to which Pinochet had committed was used against him.

Why did Pinochet make a commitment to the punishment of torture when he himself ruled with an overly strong hand? Given his behavior, it does not appear to be because he had internalized the view that torture was wrong. And while the anti-torture convention arguably benefited many people around the globe, the benefits did not outweigh the costs for Pinochet. Instead his commitment to the convention contributed to his ruin. As described in the last chapter, interdependence can enhance the benefits of sanctioning. But, in Pinochet's case, any possible enhanced benefits do not appear to have compensated for his costs.

Why, then, did he sign on to the convention? Pinochet's actions raise the question of why people enforce norms when the personal costs of doing so outweigh the benefits that they might receive from eliminating a harmful behavior. In this chapter, I describe a mechanism that helps to answer this question and that also explains why an individual might choose to sanction rather than simply free-ride on others' efforts.

Metanorms and Norm Enforcement

I have argued that when people are dependent on others for things that they want and need, they may benefit from improvement in others' welfare. The indirect benefits that flow through relationships increase the incentives to sanction, thereby encouraging norm enforcement. But dependence has further implications for norms.

An individual is motivated to try to get others to treat him well. He wants them to cooperate with him. To encourage them to do so, the individual needs to demonstrate that he is a good person—that he would be a good person with whom to interact (Posner 2000; see also Goffman 1959; and McAdams 1997). Therefore, the individual will try to behave in ways that will maintain relationships and lead others to treat him positively rather than negatively. He will try to avoid behaviors that will get him fired or lose friends.

What can people do to demonstrate that they are good exchange partners and good group members? One thing they can do is follow norms. When individuals obey group norms, they demonstrate that they know how to behave. Their actions provide evidence of their reliability and trustworthiness. We have more confidence in rulers who treat their citizens fairly than in those who do not. We have more trust in people who are consistently honest than in those who break the rules. And we are more likely to see someone as "one of us" if he wears the right clothes and speaks in the right way.

In addition to following norms, people can enforce them. If an individual punishes behavior that other group members would like to see sanctioned, then he is demonstrating that he understands what the group norms are. Further, he is providing evidence of his commitment to the norm. He is proving that he is willing to bear personal costs to enforce it (Posner 2000). And he is showing that he is not just a poser—imitating others for the sake of popularity (Centola, Willer, and Macy 2005). Teens may listen to the same music as their peers to show how cool they are, but they provide even stronger evidence of their good taste when they publicly criticize the uncool music choices of others. People demonstrate a commitment to honesty when they themselves are honest, but they also demonstrate that commitment when they punish deceit, blow the whistle on bad behavior in the workplace, and so forth.

Individuals who want to be treated well need to consider how their actions—including their sanctioning behavior—will be seen by those around them. When thinking about enforcing a norm, they will take into account the costs (potential retaliation, emotional discomfort, and so forth) and the benefits (including a reduction in deviant behavior).[1] But they will also consider how others are likely to view their sanctioning activity. They anticipate potential reactions. In other words, they pay attention to metanorms.

Metanorms are a particular kind of norm that regulate sanctioning (Axelrod 1986; Coleman 1990). They reward those who appropriately punish deviance. When President George W. Bush visited the United Nations shortly after the U.S. invasion of Iraq in 2003, he was sharply criticized by French President Jacques Chirac. Chirac's criticism can be seen as enforcement of an international norm that nations ought to work together to solve global problems. Chirac's remarks were vigorously applauded by others in the room. That applause was a form of metanorm enforcement—a reward given to someone who sanctioned a norm violator. Such rewards increase the incentives for individuals to sanction, leading in turn to stronger norms.

Importantly, the incentives provided by metanorms are selective—given only to the sanctioner. When all group members experience benefits resulting from punishment, but only the sanctioner bears the cost, then everyone has a temptation to free-ride. Everyone hopes that someone else will confront the invader, or the smoker, or the person who cuts into line. Metanorms can overcome that temptation because only the individual who punishes receives rewards. Sanctioners receive specific rewards directed at them and not to everyone else. When someone chastises a smoker, everyone benefits, but only the person who speaks up gets praise from others. When men enforce norms protecting women, many people are better off, but only men who take action are rewarded for being good guys. When Chirac criticized Bush, he was expressing the views of many in the international community, but only he was applauded. When such selective rewards are strong enough, they can offset sanctioning costs sufficiently to motivate even self-interested actors to sanction.

Metanorms are a source of incentives that can help us understand why people punish deviance even when the objective costs of doing so are bigger than the individual's share of the benefits. Metanorms provide rewards that can help to offset those costs. The desire to be seen as cool may motivate teenagers to be cruel to the unfashionable peer who likes the wrong music. Approval from the international community likely encouraged Chirac.

Why did Pinochet sign on to the anti-torture convention—something that appeared to be completely counter to his self-interest? The theory described in this chapter suggests that, like other self-interested actors, Pinochet cared about the potential reactions of others. As one participant in the convention negotiations, Swedish diplomat Hans Danelius, said, "[N]o government would wish to give the impression of preventing or obstructing the successful termination of the work. . . . This could indeed give rise to unpleasant internal or external criticism" (Hawkins 2004, 793). Apparently, even dictators sometimes care about what others think.

But if metanorms explain norm enforcement, then we need to understand metanorms themselves. We need to explain why people enforce them—why they react more positively to those who punish deviance than to those who do not. One possibility is that they want to see deviance punished; they are motivated by the consequences of behavior

(Coleman 1990). I offer a different explanation: I argue that metanorm enforcers are motivated by their social relations.

Explaining Metanorms

The Mormon church[2] is headquartered in Salt Lake City, Utah. About one and a half million Mormons live in the state. More than eleven million others are spread around the world (Ballard 2007; "Rise and Fall" 2005). They frequently come to "Zion" either to visit or to stay permanently. When they do, they are sometimes disappointed. They may complain that Mormons in Utah "take the church for granted," are not committed, or are lax in their observance. But these perceptions are inconsistent with the facts. Mormons in Utah actually comply more with church rules than those elsewhere. Consistent with its pronatalist doctrine, for example, Mormons have larger families than the average American (Heaton and Calkins 1983). But Mormons in Salt Lake City have larger families than Mormons elsewhere (Pitcher, Kunz, and Peterson 1974).[3] All young men are expected to become lay priests, but those in Utah are ordained at higher rates than those outside the state (Young 1994; see also Phillips 1998). If the rules are the same and official reactions to violations follow the dictates of church policy pronounced by the hierarchy, why does behavior vary? And if compliance is higher in Utah, why do Mormon visitors to the state sometimes complain of low commitment?

Mormons in Utah communities are surrounded by fellow Mormons— their employers and employees, their clients and customers, their doctors and nannies, and their children's teachers and friends. This means that church members living in Utah are more dependent on each other than those living elsewhere. A Mormon in New York City might depend on fellow congregants for spiritual support, but he is unlikely to run into them in other important areas of his life. By contrast, Mormons in Utah depend on their fellow Mormons every day (Phillips 2008).

This variation in dependence has implications for metanorms. People receive more support for sanctioning when they are embedded in interdependent relationships than when they are not.

Why is this so? In highly interdependent communities, people value their relationships with each other—*including their relationships with the sanctioner.* Because they value those relationships, they want to maintain them. They therefore have reason to treat the sanctioner well.[4]

Sanctioners may be particularly needy. If an individual criticizes friends or family for lack of religious observance, he may well alienate them. Others who make very costly sanctioning efforts—rape victims who testify against the perpetrator or mothers who fight against drunk driving—lose time, sleep, and emotional energy. These sanctioners may have little left to give.

Why do friends, family, and colleagues support a sanctioner who may be unable to reciprocate (at least in the short run)? Giving such support can be draining. It might appear more sensible, therefore, to interact with others—with people who have not experienced the costs of responding to deviance and who therefore can reciprocate. Why support the estranged son, the rape victim, or the consumed mother?

Because no one, including sanctioners, wants just a fair-weather friend. Everyone maintains relationships that support them at some times but make demands on them at others. If people want to maintain relationships, then they stick with their friends and family through hard times as well as good—the times when they have little to offer as well as the times when they provide much needed support.

The same thing is true of relationships with sanctioners. Individuals support the sanctioner because they value the relationship. If they fail to be supportive, and some other group member remains loyal, then in the future the sanctioner is likely to defect to this more faithful acquaintance. If individuals treat all their exchange partners who are temporarily short of resources in this way, they eventually will run out of people with whom to interact. In a sense individuals are competing with other group members for relationships. To ensure the survival of a relationship, they must continue to supply support.

This motivation to maintain ties is stronger when a relationship is valued. The more dependent people are on a sanctioner, the more they will want to support him. A rape victim pressing charges will have more social support if she has a circle of family and friends who value her. So too will a mother fighting drunk driving or a teenager making fun of music choices or an individual estranged from his family. Metanorms are stronger in groups in which people are interdependent. In such groups, individuals who sanction receive more support. In turn, deviance is more likely to be punished.

This argument suggests that interdependence among Mormons in Utah strengthens metanorms.[5] People who want to maintain valued relationships support norm enforcers. And these enforcement efforts affect behavior. Actions therefore may vary, even as beliefs remain the same. These dynamics help to explain why high rates of compliance in the Mormon cultural core might coexist with perceptions of low commitment. Visitors may perceive a greater gap between personal belief and behavior than they do in their own congregations in the hinterland.

Observations of other religious groups are consistent with the argument described here. For example, Ellison and Sherkat (1995, 1999) note that regardless of their personal feelings about church, blacks in the rural south are more likely to be active members than those elsewhere. Why? Because they have very few opportunities outside the church. In the terms used here, they are more dependent on their fellow church goers. This dependence leads to stronger metanorms and norms, and in turn, to greater activity. Consistent with the argument in this book, Ellison and Sherkat (1995) conclude that black church participation in the rural south is driven by norms and expectations, whereas participation elsewhere reflects individual preferences (p. 1416).

Dependence strengthens metanorms. Dependence and metanorms increase norm enforcement. This argument comes with a caveat, however. People want deviance to be punished, but they also want to engage in beneficial interactions. If there is a trade-off between these two goals, increases in interdependence might lead individuals to use more of their resources in interactions than in norm-related activity. When norm enforcement facilitates interaction, however, there is no trade-off. In other words, as described in the previous chapter, enforcement can produce indirect benefits. The potentially depressive effect of interdependence is offset if norm enforcement produces benefits that enhance rather than detract from the ability of individuals to engage in productive exchange.

Such indirect benefits can take a variety of forms. In the experiments in the previous chapter, sanctioning increased the resources available for exchange. Sanctioning may also create indirect benefits when it increases predictability. In the Mormon example, norm enforcement facilitates interaction in part because it clarifies the identity of actors and the rules they follow. It is easier to interact with others if you know how they are likely to behave. When norms are enforced, people are more predictable and interactions go more smoothly.

In sum, when people expect others to react positively to their sanctioning efforts, they are more likely to enforce norms. Such positive reactions are stronger in groups in which people are dependent on each other for things they want and need. In groups in which people are interdependent, therefore, we would expect to see more support for sanctioners and, in turn, more norm enforcement.[6]

The Metanorms Game

To test the theoretical predictions, I created a new Metanorms Game. Whereas in the Norms Game subjects made decisions about donating to the group and punishing those who failed to donate, in the Metanorms Game they made decisions about punishing deviance and rewarding others who punished.

Subjects were told that they were participating in groups of five. In actuality, one of the five participants was a computer-simulated actor that made money by stealing. On each round, the computer-simulated thief could steal from one person, or from nobody. Every participant (even if not a victim on a particular round) knew that he could be hurt by theft at some point and, therefore, had reason to want theft discouraged.

On each round after the thief decided whether to steal, the victim had a chance to respond. The victim could punish the thief or do nothing. Punishing was costly. If the victim chose to punish, he had to pay to do so. The sanction also inflicted a cost on the thief; when punished, the thief lost points. In addition, all four participants (including the sanctioner) benefited—they received points. The more frequently victims were punished, the higher the sanctioning rate for the group.

After the victim decided whether or not to punish the thief, everyone had an opportunity to give points to each other. When deciding how many points to give, they could consider how the victim had treated the thief. The difference between what participants gave to victims who sanctioned and what they gave to those who did not sanction provided an indicator of metanorms—support for sanctioning.

Experiment 3

In Experiment 3, I used the Metanorms Game to look at whether metanorms are stronger (that is, individuals give more support for sanctioning) in groups in which people are interdependent. I also looked at the effect of metanorms on sanctioning rates.

I manipulated two experimental conditions—interdependence and indirect benefit (see Table 3.1 for a summary of the experimental conditions). I varied interdependence by changing the value of points received from others. When people were highly interdependent, points that they received from others were worth three times their own. Participants could earn more if they exchanged than if they did not. When interdependence was low, points that people received from others were worth the same as their own. There was little reason to exchange. I also manipulated the presence or absence of an indirect benefit.

The results show that when people were interdependent, they gave more support to sanctioners. That is, interdependence strengthened metanorms. Consistent with the theory, this was true only when sanctioning produced an indirect benefit (Table 3.2 and Model 1 in Table 3.3).[7]

Interdependence also affected norm enforcement. People sanctioned most frequently when interdependence was high (and norm enforcement produced indirect benefits) (Table 3.2 and Model 2 in Table 3.3).[8]

TABLE 3.1 Experiment 3 conditions

	No Indirect Benefit	*Indirect Benefit*
Low Interdependence	1:1 No Indirect	1:1 Indirect
High Interdependence	1:3 No Indirect	1:3 Indirect

SOURCE: Based on research published in "Collective Benefits, Exchange Interests, and Norm Enforcement." *Social Forces* 82(3): 1037–62 (2004).
NOTE: I ran fourteen groups of four in each condition, for a total of fifty-six groups.

TABLE 3.2 Mean norm and metanorm enforcement across interdependence and indirect benefit conditions

		No Indirect Benefit		Indirect Benefit	
		Mean	*SD*	*Mean*	*SD*
Low Interdependence	Metanorm Enforcement	3.19	(1.58)	2.82	(1.43)
	Norm Enforcement	.745	(.149)	.690	(.182)
High Interdependence	Metanorm Enforcement	2.58[a]	(2.81)	5.47[a]	(1.96)
	Norm Enforcement	.597	(.293)	.898	(.136)

SOURCE: Drawn from "Collective Benefits, Exchange Interests, and Norm Enforcement." *Social Forces* 82(3): 1037–62 (2004).
NOTE: $N=14$ in each condition except where noted.
[a]$N=13$.

TABLE 3.3 OLS regression for the effects of interdependence and indirect benefits on metanorm and norm enforcement

	Metanorm Enforcement		Norm Enforcement			
	Model 1[a]		Model 2[b]		Model 3[a]	
Intercept	3.19****	(.535)	.745****	(.0535)	.631****	(.0640)
Interdependence	−.609	(.771)	−1.48	(.0756)	−.157*	(.0709)
Indirect Benefit	−.370	(.756)	−.0543	(.0756)	−.0412	(.0693)
Interdependence × Indirect Benefit	3.27***	(1.09)	.356***	(.107)	.263*	(.108)
Metanorms	——		——		.0356**	(.0129)
R-Square	.26		.24		.37	

SOURCE: Drawn from "Collective Benefits, Exchange Interests, and Norm Enforcement." *Social Forces* 82(3): 1037–62 (2004).
NOTE: Standard errors are in parentheses.
[a]$N=54$.
[b]$N=56$.
*$p<.05$, **$p<.01$, ***$p<.005$, ****$p<.0001$ (two-tailed tests)

Finally, when metanorms were strong, people were more likely to sanction.[9] Stronger metanorms were associated with higher rates of punishment (Model 3 in Table 3.3).[10]

In sum, the results show that interdependence increased the support given to sanctioners. That is, it strengthened metanorms. Interdependence and metanorms both affected norm enforcement.

Rewards, Punishments, and the Problem of Infinite Regress

These findings point to the importance of metanorms as part of the explanation for sanctioning. Some scholars suggest that the metanorms concept is not useful because it simply creates one more thing to explain; it creates a problem of infinite regress. If metanorms help us understand why people punish deviance, then one has to explain why they enforce metanorms. In turn, one has to explain why they enforce the enforcement of metanorms, why they enforce the enforcement of the enforcement of metanorms, and so forth. The explanation presented in this chapter avoids the infinite regress problem.

Part of the reason lies in the difference between punishing and rewarding. Punishing creates the risk of retaliation. Rewarding encourages a future return of rewards. This means that when people enforce metanorms by rewarding, they do not need support from third parties to offset their costs. Rather, they anticipate future positive exchanges with the sanctioner. Thus the potential infinite regress stops at metanorm enforcement. Note that the infinite regress could stop earlier—at the norm enforcement level—if enforcement involved rewarding good behavior rather than punishing bad acts.

One reason scholars focus on punishment is that people generally comply with norms more than they violate them. It is arguably more efficient to punish rare instances of deviance than to reward the many actors who usually obey (Oliver 1980). The theory described in this chapter suggests that this argument is not the whole story. People might well want to reward those who comply with norms (rather than just punish those who disobey) because they will get future reciprocal rewards. Consider, for example, norms about alcohol consumption. In some social groups, individuals may be punished for abstinence, but they are also rewarded for drinking. Such rewarding is especially likely to occur in tight-knit groups. My undergraduate research assistant spent a year visiting such a group—a fraternity. She attended fraternity parties and observed conversations about drinking. Her field notes describe many instances of fraternity members rewarding each other for consumption (Horne, Paulson, and Anthony 2008):

> When a member said he was going to chug an Irish Carbomb, another responded, "What a champ!"

> A member asked if he could do a beer bong. Another replied, "Hell yeah! Get in here!" When the member finished, everyone gave him a high five and cheered him.

> After a member finished a beer bong, another said, "Thata boy!"

In each of these incidents, people who drank were rewarded. Those who gave approving comments to their fraternity brothers were more likely to strengthen than to weaken their relationships. They had good reason to want to reward their drinking comrades.

We might expect to see similar dynamics in other tight-knit groups. For example, in white power groups members give positive enforcement to each other for racist declarations and tattoos (Futrell and Simi 2004). They respond positively to others' tough talk about beating up people and killing them. It costs nothing to give this kind of reward and, in fact, can lead to reciprocal approval. These dynamics can encourage high levels of hostile talk and action.

In my research I found that people reward individuals who enforce norms. But, they may also reward those who comply with norms. Such rewards are self-reinforcing because they increase the likelihood of future positive interactions.[11] Thus, when people are interdependent, they can maintain strong norms through rewarding as well as punishing. Rewards are a potentially important, yet little studied, component of norm enforcement. While this book's focus is on explaining punishment, the argument about people rewarding punishment may be extended to explain individuals rewarding compliance.

Discussion

Why did Pinochet commit to a sanctioning mechanism that later came back to hurt him? The argument developed in this chapter suggests that he did so because of metanorms. Like most people, Pinochet was motivated, to some extent, by concern with the reactions of others.

Why might a visitor perceive Mormons in Utah as less committed than those elsewhere, even though members in the heartland are actually more compliant? Higher levels of interdependence affect metanorms that in turn influence social sanctions. Thus, in Utah, more than in other places, compliance with church guidelines is motivated not just by belief, but also by strong norms.

The results in this chapter are consistent with the argument that interdependence strengthens metanorms. People who value their relationships with sanctioners support them; only sanctioners receive this support.

Social rewards (and expectations of rewards) increase people's willingness to punish deviance. Rewards encourage people to punish rather than free-ride. They help to explain why an individual may enforce norms even when the personal costs to him outweigh the benefits he receives. When metanorms are operating, social rewards can help to compensate for those costs. Metanorms provide a reason to sanction. They also create incentives (along with any indirect benefits) to enforce benevolent norms.

This chapter has looked at situations in which the individual experiences costs, but the group as a whole is better off when sanctioning occurs. Whereas Pinochet suffered because of his commitment to the anti-torture convention, around the globe people benefited (though, as I've suggested, Pinochet was not thinking about those benefits, but rather about his own reputation). In other instances, however, people enforce norms even when the aggregate benefits appear small relative to the costs—when the group would actually be better off if the norm was not enforced. Why do individuals enforce norms when doing so is not only costly for them but also reduces group welfare? In the next chapter, I extend the metanorms argument to address this question.

4   More on Metanorms

Political Correctness and the Excesses of Control

A BRITISH WEB SITE[1] REPORTS THE FOLLOWING:

We had a display of children's art and crafts at the school ...
which included pictures of people at work with a short description written below. I saw that there were many uncorrected spell-
ing, punctuation and grammatical mistakes and asked one of the
teachers (just by the by) why they had not been corrected. "So as
not to discourage them," was the reply made in the most caring
voice. Then I came to a picture by a little lad which he had entitled
"A fireman." "Fireman" had been crossed out and replaced with
"Fire Fighter."

I ... was asked if I would like a drink to which I replied, "Yes, I
will have a black coffee." The reply was, "You mean without milk?"
"Yes, that's right—black," was my response. But I was told that I
could not say this as it was racially offensive.

As I was visiting a play school to pick up my second cousin ([age]
4) on the Isle of Wight, I saw her having an argument with another

small girl by the door. She was trying to snatch a spade from the sand-pit from the other child. I approached her, and said, "Stop that, don't be naughty!" . . . in an attempt to distract her attention and keep the peace. At that point, one of the playschool carers rushed over to me and took me to one side saying "You should know better! Saying 'naughty' upsets the child and brings down their self-confidence. A child is not 'naughty,' it is using 'challenging behavior.'"

These vignettes describe the enforcement of "politically correct" ideas about gender, race, and children.[2] We can probably all think of similar instances of punishments directed against politically incorrect speech and actions—punishments that seem excessive given the stakes.

Other kinds of behaviors also appear to attract more attention than they deserve. Why, for example, have human beings at times put great effort into pursuing witches? Why do Americans sanction neighbors with brown or weedy lawns, or with clotheslines in their backyards (Heckathorn 1990, 377)?

One possibility is that people have different perceptions of the costs and benefits of sanctioning efforts. Those who pursued witches may have believed that witches were a great threat. Opponents of brown lawns and clotheslines may worry about property values. Participants may perceive sanctioning benefits that the outside observer does not.

But people also may enforce norms even when they do not believe that doing so will be beneficial. In some situations, the costs of sanctioning do not outweigh the aggregate benefits to the group as a whole—sanctioning is counterproductive.[3] Under such conditions, why do people punish? Why do they overenforce norms?

The Overenforcement of Norms

According to the consequentialist view, people do not like harmful behavior. They react negatively to it. And they direct stronger punishments against activities with more damaging consequences. They react more negatively to thefts that result in injury than they do to those that only affect the victim's pocketbook.

The implication of this view is that people pay attention to the costs and benefits of sanctioning. As the benefits of eliminating deviance increase, people are more likely to punish. As the costs go up, they are less likely to do so. If a single confrontation with a local player will have a substantial impact on crime in a neighborhood, people will be more motivated to sanction than if continual efforts would have to be made with a variety of dangerous actors. If the result of speaking out against bad behavior will be vicious counterattacks, people will be less likely to take action than if they think a deviant will accept chastisement with grace. If challenges to people asking for black coffee are met with high levels of hostility, enforcement efforts are likely to decline.

The consequentialist approach suggests that people may underenforce norms because they want to avoid personal losses and hope that others will take action instead. There is, however, no reason to expect overenforcement. This is because if people decide to sanction, they will do so only as long as their share of the resulting benefit outweighs their personal costs. They will be reluctant to continually expose themselves to counterattacks if their efforts have little positive effect. Once the costs to the individual exceed his benefits, norm enforcement will decline.

As I argued in Chapter 2, social relations can increase the benefits of sanctioning. They do so by magnifying the positive consequences of norm enforcement. When people depend on others, they gain not only from their share of the benefits, but also from the well-being of those others. People who normally would not make the effort to sanction may do so if their actions would help people close to them—their family members, neighbors, or coworkers.

This argument still suggests a limit to sanctioning, however. People might punish more than the direct benefits alone would justify, but they will stop sanctioning once the costs outweigh the combined direct and indirect benefits.

Thus the behavior consequences approach, even augmented with social considerations, implies that there will be at least some rough correlation between sanctioning costs and benefits and enforcement efforts. But if this is the case, then why do people enforce too much? Why does enforcement often appear inconsistent with obvious incentives?

Metanorms may provide an answer. If metanorm enforcement simply reflects sanctioning costs and benefits, then it will produce norms roughly consistent with them, and norms will tend to enhance group welfare. If, however, metanorms are out of sync with those incentives, then they may provide an explanation for the overenforcement that we observe. The question then is this: What is the connection between metanorm enforcement and sanctioning costs and benefits?

Behavior Consequences and Metanorm Enforcement

According to the behavior consequences logic, the effect of sanctioning benefits on metanorms is straightforward. As the gains from enforcement increase, people give more support to individuals who make sanctioning efforts. They do this because they want to receive a share of those gains. We would, therefore, expect sanctioning benefits to strengthen metanorm enforcement (Coleman 1990). People will give support to enforcers of politically correct norms, so long as those norms produce positive effects (like reducing discrimination). If such norms do not have a positive impact, however, then—on this view—enforcers will receive little reward. In other words, the larger the benefits, the stronger the metanorms and the more likely sanctioning is to occur.

The consequentialist prediction regarding the effect of sanctioning cost on metanorms is less straightforward. Group members experience the benefit of sanctioning but not the burden (which is borne only by the punisher). However, people may pay attention to costs to the extent that compensating the sanctioner will encourage him to take action. People might be willing to say something appreciative to someone who asks a smoker to stop or who tells the individual who cuts into line where to go. They do this because they enjoy cleaner air or a shorter wait in line.

How do group members determine how much support to give? The simplest procedure is for them to divide the sanctioner's cost among themselves (Coleman 1990). What happens as costs increase? Suppose, for example, that the smoker or line-cutter becomes belligerent or abusive. Group members need to give more in order to ensure that sanctioning happens. But as costs get higher, the likelihood that everyone will give rather than free-ride declines. If it takes too much effort to reward the sanctioner, people will not do it. Further, those who reward run the risk that others will not. This risk grows as the temptation to hold back increases. And that temptation rises with the costs. As the payoff decreases, rewarding may just not be worth the effort.

This argument suggests that increases in sanctioning costs will reduce support for norm enforcement. The more retaliation from the deviant, the less likely people are to give sufficient support to sanctioners. Because metanorms are not strong enough to encourage people to undertake costly enforcement efforts, sanctioning will fade. As a result, costly norms will not be maintained. We would expect that as reactions from irate customers become increasingly hostile, coworkers will provide less support to those who regulate appropriate coffee language. The enforcement of politically correct norms will decline.

Interdependence and Metanorm Enforcement

The relational theory of norm enforcement leads to a different conclusion. People enforce metanorms because they care about their social ties. To maintain relationships, people need to give not only when another has something to return, but also when the other person experiences costs and is less able to engage in exchange. In other words, if people want to maintain a relationship over the long run, they cannot be just fair-weather friends. When those with whom they interact experience costs, they will respond accordingly. The larger the cost, the more the individual will give in support.[4] We give more support to someone who is hospitalized as the result of being mugged (we visit, send cards and flowers, and so forth) than we do to someone who merely was knocked down but is physically unharmed.

The same is true when people incur costs as a result of sanctioning. All else being equal, we give more support to someone who was beat up when he interfered with a mugging attempt than we do to someone who was just shoved aside.

How do people know whether a cost is "larger" or "smaller" and whether they should provide more or less support? They compare costs with other costs. People compare the abusiveness of a deviant to the abusiveness of others with whom they have had experience. They evaluate the nastiness of a customer in comparison with the nastiness of other customers. The more retaliation that sanctioners experience, the more sympathetic their friends. The more effort sanctioners expend, the more support they will get.

This logic leads to the conclusion that as the costs of norm enforcement increase, people give *larger* rewards to sanctioners. People will give more support to a valued coworker who had to deal with a very aggressive customer than they will give to a coworker whose customer was only mildly irritated at being instructed to ask for coffee without milk.

A relational approach suggests that metanorm enforcement is not necessarily consistent with sanctioning costs and benefits. That is, sanctioning costs increase rather than decrease rewards. And those rewards encourage sanctioning. Accordingly, to the extent that people care about maintaining relationships, rewards will reflect social concerns rather than the costs of punishment. The implication is that metanorms do not necessarily lead people to enforce norms that make sense. They may encourage people to punish even when the costs of doing so are greater than the aggregate benefit—and the group as a whole is worse off as a result. Norm enforcement may be inconsistent with sanctioning costs and benefits. It may actually reduce group welfare.

Consider again the political correctness example. Racism and sexism create clear costs. The consequentialist approach would, therefore, lead us to expect negative reactions to racist and sexist behaviors. As understanding of discrimination increased, people would begin to criticize not only overt discrimination, but also its more subtle forms. But why would criticisms in some cases become out of sync with the harm caused by a behavior—as when people forbid others to use the word *black* to describe coffee without milk?[5]

People in many social circles have good reason to expect negative reactions to racist or sexist actions. The relational theory of norms suggests that they will therefore want to demonstrate that they are not racist or sexist.[6] The safest course of action is to avoid anything that might possibly appear prejudiced. And a powerful way to assert one's non-racist and non-sexist bona fides is to criticize even the slightest hint of bad behavior. Friends will, in turn, reward such criticisms.

While enforcing norms may produce benefits, social rewards can provide further incentive to sanction, leading people to react excessively to behaviors that create little damage. In Europe centuries ago, there may have been some benefit to punishing witches (Harris 1989), but an individual was also better off if she could demonstrate to others that she was not a witch. One way to do this was to punish others for potentially witchy behavior.

Social relations can lead people to punish witches, neighbors with brown lawns, or people who ask for black coffee. The cost of this sanctioning may outweigh the collective benefits to the group. People continue to sanction, however, because of social reactions.

The Experiments

I used the Metanorms Game to test the argument. Experiments 4, 5, and 6 examined the effects of sanctioning benefits and costs on metanorm and norm enforcement.

Experiment 4: Sanctioning Benefits and Interdependence

Experiment 4 focused on benefits (see Table 4.1 for a summary of the experimental conditions). I manipulated the benefit of sanctioning by changing the number of points that each group member received if the thief was punished (either 3 or 9 points). As in Experiment 3, I also manipulated interdependence. In all conditions, a subject who decided to sanction lost 20 points.

The results are not consistent with the consequentialist logic. Whereas a look at the means suggests that metanorms were stronger

TABLE 4.1 Experiment 4 conditions

	Small Benefit	*Large Benefit*
Low Interdependence	1:1 3 points	1:1 9 points
High Interdependence	1:3 3 points	1:3 9 points

SOURCE: Based on research published in "Explaining Norm Enforcement," *Rationality and Society* 19(2): 139–70 (2007).
NOTE: I ran ten groups of four in each condition for a total of forty groups.

TABLE 4.2 Mean norm and metanorm enforcement across interdependence and benefit conditions

		Small Benefit		*Large Benefit*	
		Mean	*SD*	*Mean*	*SD*
Low Interdependence	Norm Enforcement	.405	(.141)	.641	(.212)
	Metanorm Enforcement	1.92	(1.53)	2.46	(1.25)
High Interdependence	Norm Enforcement	.736	(.179)	.809	(.133)
	Metanorm Enforcement	3.32	(2.47)	4.98[a]	(2.82)

SOURCE: Drawn from "Explaining Norm Enforcement," *Rationality and Society* 19(2): 139–70 (2007).
NOTE: $N=10$ unless noted.
[a]$N=9$.

TABLE 4.3 OLS regression for the effects of benefits and interdependence on metanorms and norm enforcement

| | Metanorm Enforcement | | Norm Enforcement | | | |
	Model 1[a]		Model 2[b]		Model 3[a]	
Intercept	1.10	(.816)	.286***	(.0846)	.217**	(.0750)
Interdependence	1.95*	(.669)	.414****	(.120)	.388****	(.103)
Benefits	.181	(.112)	.0394***	(.0126)	.0356***	(.0109)
Interdependence× Benefits	——		−.0273	(.0178)	−.0387*	(.0157)
Metanorms	——		——		.0422****	(.0117)
R-Square	.23		.47		.61	

SOURCE: Drawn from "Explaining Norm Enforcement," *Rationality and Society* 19(2): 139–70 (2007).
NOTE: Standard errors are in parentheses.
[a]$N=39$.
[b]$N=40$.
*p<.05, **p<.01, ***p<.005, ****p<.001 (two-tailed tests)

when the benefits of sanctioning were larger (Table 4.2), statistical analysis does not support this conclusion. The apparent effect was not statistically significant (Model 1 in Table 4.3).

Metanorms did affect norm enforcement, however. Further, norm enforcement was affected not only by metanorms, but also by sanctioning benefits and interdependence (Models 2 and 3 in Table 4.3). People were more likely to punish when the benefits of doing so were large, but that tendency was weaker in interdependent groups (Model 3 in Table 4.3). That is, when group members were dependent on each other, the size of the sanctioning benefit had little relation to norm enforcement.[7] This finding suggests that social relations may encourage people to punish deviance even when the direct sanctioning benefits are too small to do so.

Experiments 5 and 6: Sanctioning Costs and Interdependence

Experiments 5 and 6 focused on sanctioning costs (see Table 4.4 for a summary of the experimental conditions). To analyze the data from the two studies, I combined them into one data set.[8]

In both experiments people received benefits (3 points) if someone punished the thief. I manipulated interdependence. I also varied

TABLE 4.4 Experiment 5 and 6 conditions

	Small Cost	Moderate Cost	Large Cost
Experiment 5			
Low Interdependence	1:1 −4 points	1:1 −10 points	
High Interdependence	1:3 −4 points	1:3 −10 points	
Experiment 6			
Low Interdependence	1:1 −4 points		1:1 −20 points
High Interdependence	1:3 −4 points		1:3 −20 points

SOURCE: Based on research published in "Explaining Norm Enforcement," *Rationality and Society* 19(2): 139–70 (2007).

NOTE: I ran ten groups in each condition for both experiments, producing forty groups in the small cost conditions, twenty in the moderate cost condition and twenty in the large cost condition.

sanctioning cost. Experiment 5 compared the effects of low (4 points) and moderate (10 points) costs. Experiment 6 compared low and high (20 points) costs. When costs were high, they were larger than the collective benefits group members received as a result of sanctioning. In this condition, punishment reduced group welfare.

All of the participants experienced two levels of cost. The behavior consequences argument predicts that metanorms will decline as sanctioning costs increase. But the relational argument suggests that increases in *relative* costs will strengthen metanorms. When people decide how much to reward a sanctioner, they consider his costs. But they do not compare (or at least they do not only compare) costs and benefits. Rather, they consider whether a particular cost is higher or lower than another one. Cost matters when people have some point of comparison. In the first half of the experiment, subjects had none. In the second half they could compare later costs with earlier ones. The theory predicts, therefore, that costs will affect metanorms in the second half of the experiment where subjects could make a comparison. In naturally occurring settings, such opportunities for comparison are ubiquitous. In the experimental setting, the opportunity must be created.

The results show that at the beginning of the experiment, metanorms look about the same regardless of the cost (Table 4.5). Statistical analyses confirm this impression (Model 1 in Table 4.6). The cost of sanctioning did not affect metanorms.

By contrast, in the second half of the experiment, cost did have an effect. Metanorms varied in response (Table 4.5 and Model 2 in Table 4.6).[9] This finding is consistent with the reasoning that when people decide how much to reward a sanctioner, they compare costs with other

TABLE 4.5 Mean norm and metanorm enforcement across interdependence and cost conditions

| | | Low Cost | | Medium Cost | | High Cost | |
		Mean	SD	Mean	SD	Mean	SD
Time 1							
Low	Norm	.770[a]	(1.25)	.668	(.177)	.405	(1.41)
Interdependence	Metanorm	1.25[a]	(1.06)	1.70	(1.01)	1.92	(1.53)
High	Norm	.800[a]	(.119)	.750	(.165)	.736	(.179)
Interdependence	Metanorm	3.63[a]	(2.48)	2.70	(2.57)	3.32	(2.47)
Time 2							
Low	Norm	.798[a]	(.135)	.550	(1.90)	.564	(.280)
Interdependence	Metanorm	1.23[b]	(2.04)	1.92[c]	(.586)	3.88	(3.09)
High	Norm	.889[a]	(.166)	.745	(.216)	.636	(1.81)
Interdependence	Metanorm	2.54	(1.88)	4.35[d]	(2.75)	3.64	(2.41)

SOURCE: Drawn from "Explaining Norm Enforcement," *Rationality and Society* 19(2): 139–70 (2007).
NOTE: $N=10$ unless noted.
[a]$N=20$.
[b]$N=18$.
[c]$N=9$.
[d]$N=8$.

TABLE 4.6 OLS regression for the effects of cost and interdependence on metanorm enforcement

| | Time 1 | | Time 2 | |
	Model 1[a]		Model 2[b]	
Intercept	1.13	(.543)	.500	(.703)
Interdependence	2.40***	(.768)	2.31*	(1.13)
Cost	.0422	(.0471)	.165**	(.0594)
Interdependence × Cost	−.0637	(.0666)	−.109	(.0893)
R-Square	.19		.18	

SOURCE: Drawn from "Explaining Norm Enforcement," *Rationality and Society* 19(2): 139–70 (2007).
NOTE: Standard errors are in parentheses.
[a]$N=80$.
[b]$N=65$.
*$p<.05$, **$p<.01$, ***$p<.005$ (two-tailed tests)

TABLE 4.7 Repeated measures analyses for the effects of cost and interdependence on norm enforcement

	Model 1[a]		Model 2[b]	
Intercept	.858***	(.0265)	.820***	(.0321)
Interdependence	.0276	(.0374)	−.0452	(.0498)
Cost	−.0202***	(.00255)	−.0204***	(.00255)
Interdependence × Cost	.00910*	(.00361)	.0124**	(.00363)
Metanorms	—		.0158*	(.00645)
−2 Res Log Likelihood	−102.5		−85.0	
AIC	−90.5		−80.9	
BIC	−76.2		−76.3	

SOURCE: Drawn from "Explaining Norm Enforcement," *Rationality and Society* 19(2): 139–70 (2007).
NOTE Standard errors are in parentheses.
[a]$N=80$.
[b]$N=65$.
*$p<.05$, **$p<.005$, ***$p<.0001$ (two-tailed tests)

costs. They care about how they look to their interaction partners. They seek to demonstrate their loyalty, giving more support when costs are higher and less when costs are lower.

Whereas costs increased the social support for sanctioners, they discouraged norm enforcement.[10] But that negative effect was weakened by interdependence (Table 4.7). In other words, interdependence led people to sanction even when the costs of doing so were high. Further, metanorms (that were themselves stronger when sanctioning costs were large) also encouraged people to punish (Model 2 in Table 4.7). Interdependence and social support led people to sanction when doing so actually reduced group welfare.

In sum, the results show that while the costs of sanctioning discourage people from punishing deviance, they also increase the amount of support that sanctioners receive. Together, interdependence and metanorms can encourage people to punish even when the costs are large and the benefits small. Concern with social relations produces norm enforcement patterns that one would not predict from looking at sanctioning costs and benefits alone.

Norms and Group Welfare

Norms are often puzzling. In order to explain them, some scholars have tried to identify ways in which norms that appear irrational actually produce beneficial outcomes. That is, scholars argue that norms (despite appearances) are functional. Why do people punish witches? Because doing so strengthens the church. Why don't Hindus eat cows? Because strictures against beef consumption preserve the animals for multiple other important uses (Harris 1989). This view has a range of implications. If norms contribute to group welfare, for example, then we ought to incorporate them into law—because groups have successfully worked out efficient rules that do not need to be reinvented.[11]

But such explanations sometimes come across as a mental game of trying, post hoc, to find a benefit, any benefit, to every norm or custom.

As Elster (1989) says, "The very ease with which such 'just-so-stories' can be told suggests that we should be skeptical about them" (p. 148). Further, it is easy to think of norms that are harmful that are vigorously enforced or those that would be useful that do not exist. Recognizing the weakness of explanations that assume that norms enhance group welfare, some scholars reject them. For another source of understanding, they turn to the irrational components of the human psyche. They argue that norms exist inside people's heads. They operate outside rationality; norms step in where rationality ends.

The work in this chapter suggests another approach. We can look at people who sanction those who ask for black coffee, or homeowners with brown lawns, or witches and conclude that those people are irrational, that they are true believers, that they follow a different "logic" than our own—and all of that may be true. But my research suggests that even purposive actors might engage in such sanctioning. They may consider more than just the consequences of a behavior or the consequences of punishing it. They also consider the likely reactions of others. Social relationships, therefore, can lead to enforcement efforts that are counterproductive. People might enforce norms that they would rather not enforce because of their connections to others. This means that even rational people can enforce norms in ways that are damaging. Norms and rationality are not necessarily antithetical.

Discussion

What does the theory suggest about why people sanction even when the costs of doing so appear to outweigh the objective benefits? Why can political correctness get out of control?

Metanorms can compensate people for the costs of sanctioning behavior that is not politically correct. Individuals who care about others' opinions will anticipate potential reactions. When those reactions are positive, people punish sexist and racist behavior. Such social rewards are likely to be forthcoming in cohesive groups—because people give support to those they value. In other words, individuals who experience sanctioning costs are rewarded by people with whom they interact. And, it appears, the more costs they incur (the more sacrifices they make), the more support they get. Thus metanorms lead people to react negatively to individuals whose behavior suggests insensitivity. These dynamics can lead to positive outcomes—reducing sexist and racist behavior—but they can also lead to excessive enforcement.

More generally, because metanorms reflect concern with social relations, they may be out of sync with sanctioning costs and benefits. In the experiments described here, sanctioning benefits had no effect on metanorms. Further, sanctioning costs actually increased metanorm enforcement—in turn, leading people to enforce even costly norms. These results suggest that metanorms can encourage individuals to punish when doing so is not justified by the consequences. They contribute to a mismatch between sanctioning costs and benefits, and actual enforcement efforts. The implication is that metanorms could lead people to enforce norms even when such enforcement does not benefit the group. The more that metanorms are driven by concerns with social relations rather than sanctioning costs and benefits, the less they reflect the harm caused by a particular behavior. Metanorms therefore could lead to excessive control.

This insight leads to a further question. If metanorms can lead people to overpunish harmful behavior, might they also lead people to sanction behavior that causes no harm at all? That is, might metanorms cause individuals to punish inconsequential actions? And if any behavior (not just that which is harmful) is potentially sanctionable, how do people know *what* to punish?

5 Metanorm Expectations

If Everybody's Doing It, Does That Make It Right?

HUMAN BEINGS ARE OMNIVORES. WE CAN, IF WE WANT, EAT ants and spiders, dogs and cats, horses and cows, mushrooms and mold. But we do not eat all of these potential foods. While some people in some places eat some of these things, others at different times and places consume different dishes. Our dietary restrictions are primarily social, not biological. Our cultures, more than our bodies, tell us what, when, and how to eat (Pollan 2006).

These cultural prescriptions may or may not be good for our health. For example, the Norse who lived in Greenland centuries ago relied heavily on their cattle and sheep. They raised cows even though doing so involved feeding them seaweed in the winter months and, in the spring, physically carrying the weakened animals out of the barns to get the first nibbles of grass. They did not eat the fish, ringed seals, and whales plentiful in the surrounding waters. In the 1400s, reduced to consuming their remaining cows and even their dogs, the last Norse colonies starved to death (Diamond 2005). Even as the Norse died, the local Inuit who ate from the sea managed to survive.

Why did the Norse rely on livestock rather than supplement their supplies with seafood (and potentially avoid starvation)? Why would people criticize me if I ate my cat but not if I ate my chicken?[1] Why do people react negatively to food choices that are perfectly reasonable in terms of nutrition?

Food restrictions are just one example of norms that regulate inconsequential behaviors (or that even encourage harmful actions). Fashion dictates are another. As Simmel (1957) notes,

> [V]ery frequently not the slightest reason can be found for the creations of fashion from the standpoint of an objective, aesthetic or other expediency. While in general our wearing apparel is really adapted to our needs, there is not a trace of expediency in the method by which fashion dictates.... Judging from the ugly and repugnant things that are sometimes in vogue, it would seem as though fashion were desirous of exhibiting its power by getting us to adopt the most atrocious things for its sake alone. (p. 543)

Why should anyone care whether an individual prefers horse or cow meat? Why should anyone be concerned about whether someone wears black or white socks with tennis shoes? Norms such as those that regulate the width of a man's tie or the utensils used at the dinner table raise the question of why people react negatively to inconsequential behavior (or why, as in the case of the Norse, they stick to arbitrary rules even when doing so is counterproductive).

What to Sanction?

I have argued that metanorms—social support for sanctioning—are a key factor in understanding why people enforce norms. I developed and tested the argument about metanorm enforcement and the relation between metanorms and norms in the context of harmful behavior. But everyday experience tells us that norms do not only discourage behaviors that hurt others; they also regulate inconsequential actions.

Metanorms may be part of the explanation. As already discussed, norm enforcement is problematic because, while everyone experiences the benefits, only the sanctioning individual bears the costs. Everyone, therefore, has an incentive to free-ride.

Metanorms change this dynamic, however. When they are operating, an individual has a reason to enforce a norm rather than wait for someone else to do so—because he wants others to react positively. People who expect to be rewarded for sanctioning are more likely to take action. When Jacques Chirac criticized George W. Bush's Iraq policy, he knew that others would support his critique. When men fight violence against women, they can reasonably expect that the women in their lives will approve. In the presence of supportive metanorms, people *want* to enforce norms because they personally receive perks as a result. Potential norm enforcers have less reason to free-ride than they otherwise would.

Metanorm enforcers do not have much reason to free-ride either. This is because they experience little if any cost. In fact, by rewarding the sanctioner, they increase the likelihood that he will treat them well in the future. Giving rewards encourages reciprocal rewards down the road. As long as people value their relationships with the sanctioner, they will be motivated to support him. Social relations reduce the temptation of both norm and metanorm enforcers to free-ride.

In turn, once the sanctioner is motivated to punish (because he expects social rewards to be forthcoming), the challenge for him is to figure out just what to attack. The individual tries to identify those behaviors others will approve or disapprove. He seeks to determine what sanctioning actions will be seen favorably. His problem is not so much to avoid sanctioning as to figure out *what* to sanction.

Behaviors that hurt group members are a good place to start. Reasonable people might well expect support for efforts to curb antisocial actions. The harm caused by a behavior is a good clue that others would react positively to punishment directed against it.[2] It therefore makes sense for individuals to punish behavior that clearly hurts others.

Often, however, behavior causes no harm, consequences are ambiguous, or people do not recognize the harm that results. In such situations, individuals need other indicators of disfavored activities. The consequentialist approach points to the harm caused by a behavior. The two other dominant approaches to norms—the typicality and meanings approaches—suggest additional sources of information.

Typicality as a Clue

There is lots of evidence that individuals observe others' activities and adjust their own behavior to conform. Further, people do not usually punish individuals for doing what everyone else does—providing reason to think that human beings approve of conformity. Does this mean that they also react negatively to nonconforming actions? Might the existence of a statistical regularity in behavior provoke people to punish deviations?

Intuitively, it makes sense that majority behaviors are connected to norms. High school cliques that ruthlessly criticize the peer who is different are the fodder for many teen movies. Resumes that do not follow standard formats are easily rejected. We can think of numerous situations in which the person who behaves in an unusual way is viewed negatively.

At least some research suggests the same conclusion. Schachter's (1951) well-known Johnny Rocco study provides some early evidence that typicality may produce sanctioning. In that experiment subjects discussed the appropriate punishment to apply to a delinquent. A confederate of the experimenter persisted in sticking to an opinion that differed from that of the group. Schachter observed how other group members treated that confederate. He found that at first, people tried to convince the confederate to change his mind. After a time, however, they stopped talking to him. The person who did not go along with the group was ostracized. Group consensus on the appropriate punishment led subjects to treat negatively those who expressed a different opinion.

Thus there is reason to think that people might sanction atypical actions. But just why might they do so? From a consequentialist perspective, such an effect would be unlikely. Actors who pay attention to the consequences of behavior would have no reason to bear the costs of sanctioning just because someone is doing something unusual.

Metanorms provide a possible explanation. The metanorms argument described in this book suggests that people will be willing to sanction atypical behavior if they expect that others will respond positively to their efforts. Why would people have such expectations?

Conformity research suggests a possible reason. It shows that people are sensitive to majority behaviors and adjust their own actions accordingly. They are particularly likely to conform when others can see them (Deutsch and Gerard 1955). Such findings suggest that behavioral regularities affect individuals' expectations regarding the actions that others are likely to approve. If everyone is doing something, it is reasonable for the individual to assume that others approve of the behavior. An actor may use others' behaviors as a clue to the kinds of actions they like and dislike (and adjust his own behavior accordingly). He may also use those behaviors to draw inferences about what others would like to see sanctioned. If so, then behavioral regularities provide individuals with information about metanorms. And metanorms provide a reason to sanction. Thus, people may engage in what appears to be irrational sanctioning activity because of their expectations of how others will react to their efforts.

There is some empirical support for this argument. Researchers report evidence that metanorms lead people to punish atypical behavior. Willer, Kuwabara, and Macy (2006) asked experiment participants to rate wines and then to evaluate (sanction) the wine ratings of others. When subject evaluations were public (they could be seen by other participants) rather than private (no one knew what the evaluation was), those subjects whose ratings conformed with the majority also sanctioned atypical ratings. Conformists punished nonconformists. The results of the study suggest that people use others' behaviors as a source of information about what to sanction when they know that those others are in a position to react to their sanctioning decisions—that is, when metanorm enforcement is possible.

The wine-tasting experiment provides evidence of the impact of metanorms. It gives us reason to believe that when metanorms are operating, we might expect the typicality of a behavior to affect norms. If people think that others will approve of punishment, then they will try to anticipate those reactions when they make their sanctioning decisions. They will not only use the typicality of behavior as an indicator of what others prefer and adjust their own action accordingly, but they will also use behavioral regularities as an indicator of what others would like to see punished. Accordingly, we would expect that changes in behavioral regularities produce changes in sanctioning.

Typical Behavior and Social Meaning

This argument makes sense, but it is not fully satisfactory. We can think of situations in which people have the ability to react to the sanctioning decisions of others (metanorms can operate), but atypical behavior is not punished. In North America, for example, we often do not sanction failures to wear a hat when it is 20 degrees below zero.[3] (Think of the American college student wearing flip-flops or sweatshirts in the winter rather than hats and boots. Nobody cares.) What is the difference between punishing a delinquent or someone with poor wine-tasting ability, and punishing someone who does not wear a winter hat?

Meanings approaches suggest one possibility. As described in Chapter 1, they hold that the meaning attached to a behavior is key for understanding norms. Often meanings scholars do not measure meaning itself. Rather, they use the typicality of a behavior as an indicator that it has become taken for granted. If a behavior is typical, some shared meaning is thought to have attached to it. Thus meanings scholars often look at patterns of behavior.

Just as meanings scholars often focus on typical behavior, typicality researchers frequently focus on socially meaningful actions. Schachter (1951) looked at appropriate punishments for delinquents. Willer, Kuwabara, and Macy (2006) looked at wine-tasting and explicitly designed their experiment to activate participants' concerns with social status. In both of these studies, people had reason to think that one behavior was better than another (delinquency is clearly socially undesirable; no one wants others to think they have poor taste in wine).

In everyday experience, punishment of atypical behavior is also directed at actions that are socially meaningful. One's clothing and music choices say something about one's identity; they are markers that convey socially relevant information. Not surprisingly, then, we observe people commenting about the fashion and music tastes of peers. When we observe people punishing atypical behavior, punishments appear to be aimed at socially meaningful actions.

Thus, research from both the typicality and meaning perspectives and our everyday experience often conflate the typicality of a behavior with its social meaning. But common actions are not necessarily socially meaningful, nor vice versa. While the two factors are often difficult to disentangle empirically, they are distinct theoretically.

It is possible that the typicality of a behavior alone is sufficient to draw people's attention to it and lead them to expect support for punishing deviates. But, given the existing research, the possibility remains that this mechanism is only activated when behavior that is typical also has some social meaning attached to it.

Sometimes the meaning of a behavior and the appropriate choice are clear. In the American South, for example, the willingness to engage in violence is an indicator of honor for white men (Cohen and Vandello 1998). People know that they need to respond to slights aggressively. In the United States more generally, the meaning of a chicken is food; the meaning of a cat is pet. People know better than to eat a cat.

At other times people know that a behavior is socially meaningful, but they do not necessarily know what the right choice is. A teenager moving to a new high school is aware that it is important to wear the right thing, but he may not know exactly what that is in the new environment. A college graduate starting a job may want to treat colleagues and superiors in an appropriate way, but he may not know how to do that in the context of the workplace as opposed to school.

People can understand that a category of behavior is socially important and still not be sure exactly what the right behavior is. One way to figure out what is socially appropriate is to watch others. The more frequent a behavior—the more that people are violent or not in response to disrespect, eat chickens or cats, wear blue or stone-washed jeans, or drink a vodka cran or whisky—the stronger the message regarding the acceptability of that behavior. In turn, people have reason to believe that punishment of deviations will be seen favorably.

As applied to the puzzling behavior of the Norse in Greenland, this argument suggests that the Norse focused on livestock rather than seafood because that is what they were used to.[4] In addition, however, it may be that food choices were socially meaningful. The local (pagan) Inuit ate seafood. Thus the meaning of seafood may have been connected to the pagan Inuit and the meaning of livestock to the Christian Norse. According to Diamond (2005), the Norse "[clung] to their European Christian image" (p. 247). Food may have been a part of that image.[5] If so, the argument here suggests that those socially meaningful food habits may have become salient and, in the highly interdependent Norse communities, deviations would have been sanctioned.

The Expectations Game

To test the predictions about how changes in typical behavior affect sanctioning, I created the Expectations Game. The game is adapted from the Willer, Kuwabara, and Macy (2006) wine-tasting study that is itself a variant of the classic Asch (1951) experiment.

In the Expectations Game, each subject participated in a group with seven simulated actors. The actors took turns making a particular choice—a choice between X and W. This decision was as arbitrary as it sounds. Subjects literally had to choose between the two letters. The X–W choice had no consequences in and of itself. It had no association with status, or aesthetic judgment, or norms, or any other evaluation outside the lab. The point here was to create an artificial behavior with no (or as little as possible) preexisting social meaning.[6] The only thing that might make X or W more socially salient was the number of simulated actors who chose it.

The actors made their X–W choices one at a time. The subject went seventh. This meant that he saw all but one actor's choice before making

X–W Choice

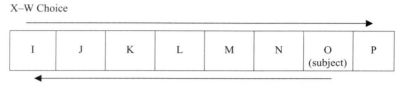

Reaction to Choices

FIGURE 5.1 Order of decisions
SOURCE: Based on research described in "Metanorm Expectations: Determining What to Sanction, *Advances in Group Processes* (Emerald Group, 2009).

his own. (For an illustration of the order in which actors made decisions, see Figure 5.1.)

After the last actor made his X–W decision, everyone reacted to each other's choices. They did this by giving other individuals between 0 and 25 points. This time, the subject went first. He had to make a sanctioning decision without knowing what anyone else would do. He knew that actors going after him would decide how many points to give to him. If others reacted negatively to his sanctioning choice, the subject would have less money to take home at the end of the experiment.

Unlike in the Metanorms Game, here participants did not enforce metanorms. Each subject had to make a sanctioning decision before seeing any metanorm enforcement. The subject therefore needed to use sources of information (such as observations of others' behavior) as a clue to how those others were likely to react to his sanctioning decision.

Experiment 7: Patterns of Behavior

Experiment 7 tested the hypothesis that variation in patterns of behavior affects sanctioning. I expected that people who conformed with the majority would punish those who deviated—that is, they would give more points to those who conformed with the majority than to those who did not.

I created two conditions—one in which X was the typical behavior and one in which W was typical (see Figure 5.2). In the X-typical condition, the majority of simulated actors (all those who preceded the subject) chose X, and only one chose W. In the W-typical condition, the

X-Typical Condition   W-Typical Condition

Person I	(X)	W
Person J	(X)	W
Person K	(X)	W
Person L	(X)	W
Person M	(X)	W
Person N	(X)	W
Person O	X	W
Person P	X	W

Person I	X	(W)
Person J	X	(W)
Person K	X	(W)
Person L	X	(W)
Person M	X	(W)
Person N	X	(W)
Person O	X	W
Person P	X	W

FIGURE 5.2 X-typical and W-typical conditions

SOURCE: Based on research described in "Metanorm Expectations: Determining What to Sanction, *Advances in Group Processes* (Emerald Group, 2009).
NOTE: This illustration of the conditions shows what a subject saw before he made the X–W choice. Each subject saw either the form with the X-typical condition or the one with the W-typical condition. I ran twenty subjects in each condition. I then analyzed the sanctioning decisions of those who conformed with the majority.

majority chose W, and one chose X. In both conditions, I measured the size of the norm discouraging people from choosing X and looked to see if the choices of the simulated actors affected subjects' enforcement of an anti-X norm. I found that there was no statistically significant difference in sanctioning across the two conditions. Subjects' sanctioning decisions were not affected by others' X–W choices.

Experiment 8: Patterns of Meaningful Behavior

I then conducted a follow-up experiment to see if variation in patterns of socially meaningful behavior affected sanctioning. The basic experimental framework was the same as in Experiment 7 except that here I modified the description of the X–W choice. I wanted to give participants some reason to think that one of the choices would be more socially desirable than the other, without explicitly telling them what that choice was. The experiment instructions said that research has revealed a surprising yet consistent finding—preferences for particular patterns of lines are associated with the number of friends that people have. Those who prefer one category of lines tend to have more friends; those who prefer the other category tend to have fewer friends. The line patterns were the letters X and W. Subjects were asked to choose one of these two line patterns. In other words, subjects had exactly the same choice as they had in Experiment 7—they had to choose between X and W. But this time they had information suggesting that their X–W choice might tell people whether they had lots of friends or only a few.

Again, I manipulated typicality—creating an X-typical and a W-typical condition. I found that in the X-typical condition subjects gave *more* to those who chose X than to those who chose W (mean difference=1.41, s.d.=3.25, n=13).[7] In the W-typical condition, they gave *less* to those who chose X than to those who chose W (mean difference=−4.63, s.d.=5.56, n=13). The difference in sanctioning across these two conditions is statistically significant ($t(24)=3.38$, $p<.005$). The results show that when the X–W choice was socially meaningful—that is, subjects had reason to think that one choice was more socially desirable than another—they punished those who did not behave in the same way as the majority.

The results of Experiments 7 and 8, in conjunction with the results of the wine-tasting study (Willer, Kuwabara, and Macy 2006), suggest that metanorms lead people to sanction atypical behavior when that behavior has some a priori socially desirable meaning. When a behavior is meaningless, typicality alone—even if metanorms can operate—may not be sufficient to produce sanctioning. In other words, typicality in and of itself does not necessarily make a behavior meaningful. Instead, when people have reason to believe that an action might have social meaning, but they are not sure what that meaning might be, they use the frequency of the behavior as a clue to its social acceptability—behaving in ways that others do and sanctioning those who do not. They do this when others can see and react to their decisions. Characteristics of behavior alone do not predict sanctioning. Metanorms are an important causal factor (Willer, Kuwabara, and Macy 2006).

It is worth noting here that while there was not a statistically significant effect of meaningless behavior on sanctioning, the correlation was in the predicted direction. It is possible that there is some tendency to react to atypical behavior that was not picked up here. Additional research should be done to investigate this possibility and the conditions under which it may or may not occur.

It may be that punishment of nonconformity varies across individuals and across cultures. We know that underlying rates of conformity vary (Milgram 1961). Further, psychological research shows that emotional reactions to different kinds of behavior vary across social groups (Haidt, Koller, and Dias 1993). For example, low-income individuals are more likely to say that someone ought to be punished for or prevented from engaging in an act that is disgusting (but not harmful) than high-income individuals. High-income people (including college students) express negative reactions to harmful behaviors but not to offensive ones—suggesting that college students are particularly unlikely to punish the (non-harmful) behaviors described in this chapter. It is possible, then, that in some subcultures, patterns of behavior alone might produce sanctioning, whereas in others, more than mere nonconformity is needed. If so, then the results of experiments using the Expectations Game setting would vary across cultural groups.

Individuals within cultures may also differ. Among my college student subjects, most conformed, but some did not. Economists find evidence that some of their subjects are self-interested while others are "strong reciprocators" who are inclined to cooperate (Fehr and Gintis 2007). We know relatively little about who these people are, however—who conforms and who does not, who cooperates and who does not. Further research should explore the causes of such individual variation and their implications for norm enforcement.

Other Sources of Clues

The results in this chapter are consistent with the argument that people rely on not just the harm caused by a behavior but also its meaning and typicality to determine what sanctioning actions others are likely to approve. The dominant approaches to norms focus on three factors— the consequences of behavior, the meaning attached to it, and the frequency with which it occurs. I have argued that these factors matter, in part, because they provide information to people about what behaviors they should sanction. Social relations and metanorms then help motivate them to actually bear the costs of punishing.

Other factors may also draw people's attention to one behavior or another. Of particular interest here, given the focus of this book on relationships, are social factors that may make a particular behavior salient.

There is lots of evidence that human beings are group-oriented creatures—that group membership is important to us. When researchers assign people to groups with only minimal differences, individuals are biased toward members of their group. Subjects assigned to groups based on their preference for Klee or Kandinsky paintings, or to "group X" or "group W" based on the flip of a coin, are more generous to in-group than out-group members (Billig and Tajfel 1973; see also Brewer 1979; Brewer and Kramer 1985; Tajfel 1982; Tajfel et al. 1971; and Turner, Brown, and Tajfel 1979).

Research also suggests that people are sensitive to differences in behavior patterns across groups (Turner et al. 1987). For example, students do not want to be too much like teachers. Teenagers distinguish themselves from their parents and other adults (Harris 1999).

People appear to be particularly sensitive to group membership in situations of intergroup conflict—where one group's success occurs at the expense of the other. Social psychological research shows that such conflicts increase in-group cohesion and cooperation (Bornstein and Ben-Yossef 1994; Sherif et al. 1988; Simmel 1955). Studies of ethnic mobilization find similar effects (Olzak 1992).

Research in evolutionary psychology suggests that intergroup conflict was an important factor in human evolution, providing further reason to think that people are sensitive to group coalitions (van der Dennen and Falger 1990). Cosmides, Tooby, and Kurzban (2003), for example, report the results of an experiment in which they showed subjects pictures of two black and two white individuals. The researchers found that if subjects saw just the individuals, they noticed race. But, when the researchers created competing teams wearing different-colored jerseys and put one white and one black person on each team, subjects no longer paid much attention to race. That is, membership in competing teams erased its effect. These findings provide further evidence of the salience of group membership in intergroup conflict situations.

A study conducted by Sherif and colleagues (1988) not only suggests that people care about group conflict but also points to a possible connection between intergroup conflict and sanctioning. In his famous Robbers Cave experiment, Sherif brought eleven- and twelve-year-old boys to summer camp. He divided them into two groups and had them engage in competitions. He found that the boys reacted negatively to members of their team who sought to alleviate the conflict and reacted positively toward fellow members who behaved aggressively toward the other team.

Despite the importance of groups and intergroup conflict, there is relatively little contemporary norms research looking at the connections between such conflict and norm enforcement. I conducted an exploratory study on the issue. I modified the Expectations Game described in this chapter to include two groups and then manipulated the presence or absence of conflict between groups. I found that when the X–W decision affected one group's outcome relative to another, people were more likely to punish atypical choices by fellow group members than they were when the X–W decision did not affect outcomes.

Additional work has been conducted by Stephen Benard, whose research suggests that people may punish fellow group members more when there is intergroup conflict than when there is not—even when the objective payoff in the two instances is the same. Benard found that intergroup conflict had different effects for different kinds of people. It increased sanctioning by individualists but decreased sanctioning by collectivists (Benard 2007a). Further, the immanence of the threat mattered (Benard 2007b). Sanctioning was affected by recent actions of the out-group. So, if out-group individuals had just done something that hurt in-group member earnings, those in-group members were more likely to sanction each other's deviant behavior.

These initial studies suggest that both individual and group level factors matter. They point to the potential importance of intergroup conflict for understanding norms and highlight the complexity of the relationship.

There are likely other social structural conditions that also affect norm enforcement. Researchers find, for example, that the association of behaviors with social status affects the extent to which individuals adopt those behaviors. Fashion is a notable example. Fashion distinguishes people, identifying the "right" folks. Individuals are motivated to adopt fashions that will align them with desirable statuses (Pesendorfer 1995; Simmel 1957; see also Elias 2000).

Do these processes produce sanctioning? The argument presented in this book suggests that they may. Behaviors that are associated with status may become socially meaningful. In turn, people who want to affirm that they have high status may sanction those who dress differently in order to affirm their own superiority. Low-status groups may well enforce opposition norms among their own members (Portes 1998). Blacks may punish those who "act white"; working-class students may punish those who try to do well in school (Fordham and Ogbu 1986; Willis 1981).

In sum, a range of social structural features may draw attention to particular behaviors and lead people to think that others would approve of sanctions directed against those behaviors. When metanorms can operate, they strengthen the incentives to sanction deviations from salient actions. To the extent that this is the case, an important part of the task of explaining norms involves identifying these salient behaviors and the social structural conditions in which they are embedded. A further task is to explain why individuals differ in their reactions to these structural conditions.

Mistakes

This chapter highlights the tendency of individuals to try to figure out what behaviors others approve or disapprove and, therefore, would like to see punished. But there is no guarantee that their reading of the clues will be correct. Decades ago, Floyd Allport coined the term "pluralistic ignorance"—the state of affairs in which individuals hold one attitude but mistakenly believe that everyone else adheres to a different one (Katz and Allport 1928). Such erroneous beliefs can lead to high levels of conformity that are inconsistent with personal preferences.

The results in this chapter suggest that pluralistic ignorance may also lead people to enforce norms in which they do not believe—providing individuals with even more evidence supporting their false impressions. Collective norms, therefore, may be very different from individual attitudes.[8]

Research shows that college students think others support heavy drinking more than they actually do, and in turn, they drink more themselves (Prentice and Miller 1993, 1996). This chapter suggests that students not only drink more, they also may punish those who do not—providing evidence that drinking is socially mandated. Such dynamics can produce widespread effects.

Debates about the American culture wars provide an example. These debates peaked in the 1980s and 1990s, but vestiges remain. In his book *Culture Wars*, James Hunter (1991) argues that there is a war in America between traditional and progressive values:

> [This] culture war emerges over fundamentally different conceptions of moral authority, over different ideas about truth, the good, obligation to one another, the nature of community, and so on. It is, therefore, cultural conflict at its deepest level. . . . [W]e come to see that the contemporary culture war is ultimately a struggle over national identity—over the meaning of America. (pp. 49–50)

Statements of political partisans reflect a similar view. For Pat Bu-chanan, "There is a religious war going on in this country, a cultural war as critical to the kind of nation we shall be as the Cold War itself, for this war is for the soul of America" (Fiorina, Abrams, and Pope 2006, 1). Journalists likewise report that "[t]he divide [goes] deeper than politics. It reache[s] into the nation's psyche. . . ." (Fiorina, Abrams, and Pope 2006, 3).

Despite this rhetoric, analyses of survey data suggest that, in fact, the differences between individuals range from minimal to nonexistent and that the gap has changed little, if any, over time (see, for example, DiMaggio, Evans, and Bryson 1996). Even research on as controversial a topic as abortion does not suggest an increase in polarization (Mouw and Sobel 2001). Further, voting patterns do not show a widening divide.[9] Thus assessments of individual attitudes lead to the conclusion that there is no culture war.

These two perspectives on America—one that sees us as deeply divided and the other as mostly middle of the road in our views—presents a puzzle. How can we have little change and little difference in individual attitudes, yet simultaneously, a perception of deep divisions and differences and what appear to be very real conflicts?

Critics suggest that because there has been little or no change in individual attitudes, there is no culture war. The relational theory of norm enforcement suggests that this conclusion may be wrong. According to the theory, people sanction in order to look good to others. This concern with social relations distorts the link between individual opinions and norms.[10] There might well be a war of norms even if there is not a war of individual values. Such a war can be real and very divisive. But, it may also be diffused—if people obtain accurate information about what others really think.

Discussion

Why would my friends react very negatively if I invited them over for a dinner of cat meat but be happy with grilled chicken? Cats are pets.

Chickens are raised for food. One cannot serve cat for dinner. Anyone criticizing a cat eater could be confident of social support.

Why did the Norse not take advantage of the fish and whales available? Part of the story may be that they did not learn the skills necessary to hunt sea life. But why not? There likely were social pressures not to do so. If the meaning of eating whale was associated with local pagan Inuit, that meaning, in conjunction with existing Norse eating habits, may very well have discouraged the Norse from exploring new food options. It would be hard for anyone to criticize a community member for spending time taking care of his cows or to react positively to someone who ate like the pagans. Such reactions would have been seen as inappropriate. The typicality of a behavior in conjunction with its meaning in the Greenland context led to damaging food norms.

Why do teenagers punish peers for bad clothing and music choices? Because those choices and criticisms of them are socially meaningful. People who want to look good to others will criticize atypical behavior in order to establish their own bona fides and to attract positive attention.

Earlier chapters focus on the consequences of behavior—showing that social relations and metanorms affect the extent to which harmful behavior is punished. This chapter looks at the meaning and typicality of behavior—demonstrating that metanorms also work in conjunction with these behavior characteristics to produce sanctioning. These findings provide evidence that, whatever the characteristics of a behavior (its consequences, frequency, or meaning), those characteristics alone do not drive norm enforcement. As the experiments described throughout the book demonstrate, metanorms matter. One reason that behavior consequences, meaning, and frequency are important for understanding norms is that they affect expectations of support for sanctions. These expectations in turn affect norm enforcement. When social relations are strong enough, metanorms have the potential to motivate people to sanction almost anything.

Thus far, I have described the relational theory of norms and a series of lab experiments testing the theoretical predictions. Given the experimental support, we can have some level of confidence in the theory.

There is reason to believe that social relations and metanorms affect norm enforcement. What can one do with such an abstract theory outside of the lab? How might it be useful to researchers interested in substantive questions for which norms might be relevant? In the next chapter, I begin to explore some possibilities.

6 Moving Out of the Lab

Sex, Crime, and Human Rights

EXPERIMENTAL WORK OFTEN OCCURS SEPARATELY FROM RE-search on particular concrete issues. Scholars interested in substantive questions read the literature in their area but may not pay much attention to abstract, experimental work. Researchers conducting experiments develop abstract theories and test them in the lab. They often say little about the implications of their work for substantive questions. But if theories tested in the lab are not useful for helping us understand naturally occurring events in the world, then they risk irrelevance.

Abstract theories tested in the lab are useful in at least three ways. First, they can produce novel substantive hypotheses. Second, they can provide insights about the mechanisms responsible for observed correlations. In turn, these insights about mechanisms have implications for the kinds of questions we ask and the data we collect. Third, and most importantly, abstract theories tested in the lab can improve our ability to explain concrete social phenomena.

In this chapter, I explore some of the implications of the relational theory of norm enforcement in three very different contexts. I use the theory to 1) develop a novel hypothesis about sex norms, 2) describe a mechanism that might help account for observed correlations between neighborhood characteristics and crime and make suggestions about data collection efforts that might help to increase our understanding of the informal control of crime, and 3) explain nations' commitment to the International Criminal Court—showing that incorporating the social concerns identified by the theory improves predictions.

Applying Abstract Theory

Applying abstract theories to concrete settings is not a straightforward task. The researcher must do two things—identify those settings in which the theory can appropriately be applied and identify empirical indicators of the theoretical concepts.

Appropriate Settings

Social science researchers often begin with an interest in a particular substantive issue—crime, or families, or human rights. They develop theories specific to those substantive interests. When testing their theories, they try to identify respondents who are representative of the population of interest. If the sample is drawn correctly, then researchers can generalize from the sample to the larger population. That is, they assume that behavior in the population will reflect the findings for the sample.

The approach for applying abstract theory is different. Abstract theories are potentially useful across a range of substantive settings. Researchers explore the validity of the theory by applying it to situations that meet the theoretical scope conditions—the conditions under which the theory is meant to apply. As Webster and Sell (2007) write, "Scope conditions tell the kinds of situations where a theory claims it can describe what happens. If a situation meets its scope conditions, the theory ought to be able to predict accurately. If a situation is outside that scope, the theory makes no claim to being able to make predictions" (p. 17). We can explore the usefulness of a theory outside the lab by testing it in a range of substantive settings that meet the scope conditions (Willer and Walker 2007).

The theory in this book is limited by several such conditions. First, it is meant to apply to situations in which there is overlap between the behavior of interest and the interaction of individuals. That is, there must be ties between people who are affected by a particular behavior, or who attach the same meaning to it, or who are exposed to the same behavioral regularities.

Second, the theory is meant to apply to situations in which people interact with each other over time. For a sanctioner to be motivated by possible rewards from others, he has to anticipate that he will be interacting with those others. And for metanorm enforcers to be motivated to reward a sanctioner, they must anticipate future interactions with him. Note that the theory does not require that people interact with the deviant over time, but rather that they expect interactions with each other. Of particular importance are relations between sanctioners and those around them.

Third, the theory is meant to apply to situations in which people have information about behaviors and sanctions. To react negatively to a behavior, people have to know about the bad act and who did it. Similarly, they must have information about sanctions and sanctioners in order to respond to them. Without this kind of knowledge, norms and metanorms cannot operate effectively. Invisible private behavior cannot be punished and invisible private sanctions cannot be rewarded.

In sum, the theory in this book should be predictive in settings in which people who have common experiences with a particular behavior interact with each other over time and in which individuals' behaviors and sanctioning efforts are visible.

Empirical Indicators

In addition to identifying appropriate conditions in which to test the theory, the researcher must translate the abstract theoretical concepts into empirical indicators that can be measured. Durkheim's *Suicide* (1951), for example, identified social integration as a factor affecting suicide rates. Integration is an abstract concept. Durkheim linked that abstract concept to empirical indicators—religion and family. He argued that Catholics were more integrated than Protestants and that married men were more integrated than single men.

When theories include abstract concepts, one must identify appropriate empirical indicators of those concepts. Doing so often requires making auxiliary assumptions that are not a part of the theory. Durkheim's argument about the relation between integration and suicide does not tell us anything about the conditions in the world under which people are more or less integrated. Durkheim had reasons other than his explanation of suicide for linking marriage and religion with integration.

The relational theory of norms is stated in abstract terms, such as costs, benefits, interdependence, norm enforcement, and metanorm enforcement. It is relatively straightforward to manipulate the costs and benefits of sanctioning or the interdependence of actors or to measure metanorm or norm enforcement in the lab. In natural settings, however, measurement is more challenging. And the theory itself does not identify appropriate indicators.

In my experiments, participants depended on each other (to varying degrees) to make money. Outside of the lab, however, people value many things other than money and need more from others than just monetary assistance. Applying the theory requires making some auxiliary assumptions about what people might value about their relationships. I need to think about what people might be dependent on others for in particular contexts.

Metanorm and norm enforcement are also difficult to measure in naturally occurring settings. I cannot see all sanctions or all reactions to sanctioners. And in many instances, statements and behaviors must be interpreted—it is not clear whether they are intended to be or are experienced as sanctions. I therefore need to identify measures that I have reason to think provide information about norm and metanorm enforcement.

Applying any abstract theory requires additional assumptions that link the abstract theory to a particular empirical context—assumptions that are not part of the theory itself. Once one determines the appropriate empirical indicators for the theoretical concepts, one can apply the theory. In this chapter I provide three examples that apply the relational theory of norms outside the lab.

Dependence: Explaining the Permissiveness of Sex Norms

Norms regulating sexual activity vary dramatically across societies. Researchers have sought to explain why. Standard arguments suggest that norms constraining heterosexual sex vary with the relative power of men and women. As Lee (1987) writes, "[T]he decision-making power of each spouse should vary directly with the resources provided by that spouse" (p. 69; see also Blood and Wolfe 1960). The more resources a partner has, the more able she or he is to control the other person and to resist the other's control efforts. Thus, when a woman is dependent on her partner for resources, she is in a weak position; she is unable to enforce her expectations and constrain his activity. The powerful male partner is in a good position to control the woman. Conversely, when a woman is relatively independent, she is more able to exert control over her male partner, and he is less able to enforce his demands.

In other words, a standard approach to understanding male-female relations suggests that as people's resources increase, their ability to control their partners' behavior—including sexual activity—grows. On this view, variation in norms regulating sexual activity is a function of actors' power to enforce their expectations. It suggests that as women's resources decline, their partners' control over their sexual activity increases. As women gain resources, they strengthen their ability to constrain their husbands' activities (Coleman 1966; Eckhardt 1971). Female dependence, therefore, leads to more regulation of women and less regulation of men.

Does the relational theory of norms make the same prediction? Before applying the theory, I discuss whether sex norms are an appropriate context in which to do so.

As described above, the relational theory of norm enforcement is meant to apply to situations in which those who are exposed to the characteristics of behavior also interact with each other, people are able to interact over time, and the behavior and the sanctions directed against that behavior are public. All of these conditions are met. People who are affected by the sexual behavior of their partners or romantic interests interact with others who are affected by those same kinds of behaviors. Further, these interactions occur over time. Women and men have colleagues as intimate relationships come and go, and they maintain friendships through the ups and downs of romance. Family members interact whether or not one of them is cheating.

In addition, at least to some extent, people have information about behavior and sanctions. Sex is a private activity. But men and women frequently find out about the cheating of their spouses. Parents learn about the behavior of their children. Sex outside of marriage can only be sanctioned if it is discovered. But often it is. People have to find time away from their parents or partners, they have to find a place to meet where they will not be seen, and so forth. These actions leave tracks that others can, and often do, discover. People are also often aware when sanctions are imposed. The "scarlet letter" is an obvious example (Hawthorne 1850), as are public beatings and humiliation. When parents disown children or spouses divorce the adulterers, those sanctions are also visible. Thus social regulation of sex is an appropriate context in which to apply the theory. What does it predict?

The key insight described in Chapter 2 is that dependence alters the benefits associated with sanctioning. When an individual is dependent on another person, he benefits from that person's resources. When norm enforcement increases those resources, the individual gains. Those gains motivate people to sanction—leading to more enforcement.

As applied to norms regulating sex, this argument suggests that when women are dependent on men, they have more incentive to enforce norms that preserve men's resources. A woman presumably does not want a man to spend his resources on other women and their children. She is better off if he remains loyal to her. We would expect, therefore, that increased female dependence would be associated with stronger norms constraining male sexual activity and encouraging monogamy. While standard approaches to male-female relations predict that increased female dependence leads women to exercise less control, the relational theory of norms predicts that it encourages them to exercise greater control over men (because the benefits of doing so are larger). A woman's father and brothers would also have reason to want their daughter or sister to be treated well by her male partner. Thus not only the woman, but also her relatives, would be more likely to sanction. This is a novel prediction that differs from traditional analyses of male-female relations.

Is there any reason to think that the prediction might be right? Here I describe the results of some early research I conducted to begin to assess this argument (Horne 2004). I applied the theory to make predictions about norms regulating male sexual activity across cultures.

To make concrete predictions, I needed to identify appropriate indicators of dependence. Anthropological research explores cultural characteristics across societies. It identifies three factors related to a woman's support from her family of origin that provide indicators of dependence: descent rules, inheritance restrictions, and marital location.

In many parts of the world, descent rules are an important feature of social organization. In patrilineal societies, property is passed down through the male line. In the less common matrilineal societies, by contrast, property passes through females. Thus, women have access to inherited resources through their own, rather than their husbands', families.

Rules regarding the extent to which women and men can inherit also differ. Whereas in some societies only male offspring may inherit real and personal property, in others both males and females may inherit from their relatives. In these communities women have additional sources of goods that contribute to their independence from their husbands.

The location of marital residence is also relevant. In patrilocal groups women leave their home of origin to move to the man's village. According to Nielsen (1978), "[T]he wife goes to live, essentially as a stranger, in the husband's home. She is often treated as a minor . . . and is under the authoritative control of her mother-in-law" (p. 30). In matrilocal societies, however, the man moves to the woman's village. Brothers, rather than husbands, have more responsibility for and rights to the children. One consequence of the matrilocal social structure is that women are not as dependent on the fathers of their children as they are in patrilocal systems. Because the wife remains in the village where her family lives, she (with the help of her family) is more able to provide for her children's needs than are women who have no property and who live with their husbands' families.

In cultures that are matrilineal or matrilocal or in which females can inherit property, women are less dependent on their male partners than they are in cultures that are patrilineal or patrilocal or in which only men can inherit. A standard approach would predict that norms regulating men will be stronger in the first than the second. By contrast, the relational theory of norms predicts the reverse. Norms regulating male sexual activity will be more permissive in societies that are matrilocal or matrilineal or allow inheritance by women and will be more restrictive in cultures that are patrilocal or patrilineal or do not allow inheritance by women.

To evaluate these predictions, I analyzed data from the Standard Cross-Cultural Sample (Murdock and White 1969). This data set includes ethnographic information for 186 cultures. Since the development of the sample, many anthropologists have coded the data for their own research. The accumulation of these coding efforts has resulted in a systematic data set that includes a range of variables. The data set has a number of indicators of marital location, descent rules, and inheritance rules. It also includes several indicators of norms—reports of sex-related rules, descriptions of sexual behavior, and information about sanctions.

Analyses of these data provide support for the predictions (see Horne 2004b). In societies that are matrilocal and in which inheritance and descent rules provide resources to women, attitudes about male premarital sex are more permissive and the consequences for males who engage in premarital sex are less severe than they are in patrilocal societies or those in which women are unable to inherit. Female dependence increases the restrictiveness of norms regulating men.

The cross-cultural data provide some initial support for the theory. The prediction regarding the relation between female dependence and sex norms could be tested in other settings as well. The reasons for dependence will not be the same in all circumstances. Thus the empirical measures will vary. Women are less dependent on their partners if they have support from their family of origin, if they are able to earn a living themselves, or if government subsidies provide an alternative source of income. These factors may vary not only across cultures but also across nations or across subgroups within a particular country. The theory could be tested using empirical indicators appropriate for these different settings.

In summary, a standard approach to thinking about male-female relations suggests that women will exert more control when they have more power (are less dependent). The relational theory of norms makes the opposite prediction. As women's dependence on their partners increases, they (and their brothers and fathers) have more interest in controlling the male partners' activity. Thus norms regulating male sexual behavior will be stronger. The insight about the connection between dependence and norms produces a novel prediction regarding sex norms that is applicable across a range of settings.

Metanorms: Explaining Variation in the Informal Control of Crime Across Neighborhoods

Theories that have been tested in the lab can provide insights regarding mechanisms and guidance for the kinds of data that we might want to collect out of the lab. Consider, for example, the problem of explaining variation in criminal activity. Criminologists have long noted that rates of crime vary across neighborhoods. That is, controlling for the traits of individuals, neighborhood characteristics affect deviant and criminal activity. But why?

Traditional explanations hold that some neighborhoods exercise more informal control than others. As Sampson, Raudenbush, and Earls (1997) write, "Social control refers generally to the capacity of a group to regulate its members according to desired principles—to realize collective . . . goals. One central goal is the desire of community residents to live in safe and orderly environments that are free of predatory crime, especially interpersonal violence" (p. 918). Neighborhoods with different characteristics have different levels of control (see, for example, Bursik and Grasmick 1993; and Sampson and Groves 1989).

But again, why? Why, for example, would having neighbors who are black or white, rich or poor, or single or married affect the likelihood that an individual would sanction bad behavior? Researchers have identified numerous correlates of crime—neighborhood income levels, racial and ethnic composition, owner-occupied homes versus rental properties, and so forth. They have developed sophisticated statistical techniques to help them parse out individual- and group-level effects. But the mechanisms responsible for these effects are less well understood.

Like criminologists, norms researchers are also interested in informal control. Informal neighborhood control of crime is a particular instance of norm enforcement. Does the relational theory of norms provide any insights?

To begin, I consider whether neighborhood crime is an appropriate issue to which to apply the theory. People living in neighborhoods are affected by criminal activity in those neighborhoods and interact with others who are similarly affected. They are able to interact with each other over time (though the length of time varies with the mobility of the neighborhood). Further, people often have information about criminal and delinquent behavior and sanctions. They know that a crime happened. They know that homes or businesses were broken into, that a neighbor was beaten up. And often they have suspicions about particular individuals. They know if a neighborhood teen is a gang member or a troublemaker. They know if someone has started hanging out with the wrong kinds of friends. Because they are aware of criminal events and suspect individuals, people are able to take action to address crime in their communities. Their actions are often visible to those around them. Thus neighborhood control of crime is an appropriate setting in which to apply the relational theory of norm enforcement.

The theory predicts that interdependence and metanorms will have a positive effect on social control efforts. My experimental results suggest that at least part of the effect of interdependence on informal control will be due to metanorms (see note 9 in Chapter 3).

John Hoffmann and I conducted some exploratory analyses to test these predictions (Horne and Hoffmann 2005). We used data collected in Chicago neighborhoods (Earls 1999). The data set provides information on a range of neighborhood- and individual-level characteristics. It also provides measures that are reasonable (though not perfect) indicators of interdependence, metanorms, and sanctioning.

One set of questions asks people for their thoughts about their neighbors—are they trustworthy, do they share the same values, and so forth. These items provide at least some data relevant for assessing the value that people place on their relationships with their neighbors, and therefore, the level of interdependence in the community. We combined these indicators into a single interdependence measure. Our statistical analyses showed that this measure was positively correlated with control efforts.

We then added a measure of metanorms to the analysis. To create this measure, we turned to questions asking respondents whether they thought their neighbors would intervene if they saw deviant behavior (such as skipping school, spray-painting graffiti, showing disrespect to an adult, or fighting). We assumed that if respondents thought their neighbors would intervene, they would also expect their neighbors to approve of intervention efforts. In essence, we disentangled the collective efficacy indicator used by Sampson and his colleagues (Sampson, Raudenbush, and Earls 1997). That measure combined two sets of survey items (our measures of interdependence and metanorms). Sampson, Raudenbush, and Earls found, consistent with their predictions, that neighborhood characteristics affected crime and that collective efficacy mediated the relation between neighborhood characteristics and crime. We disentangled the collective efficacy measure in order to try to explain control. We wanted to see if interdependence and metanorms affected control and if metanorms mediated the effect of interdependence on control.

Consistent with the prediction, the relation between interdependence and control was mediated by metanorms. Metanorms had a positive, statistically significant effect on informal control. We interpret these initial analyses as supporting the relational theory of norms.

The measures we used are not perfect, of course. But it may be fruitful to test the theory using more appropriate measures of interdependence, metanorms, and sanctioning. One approach would be to directly ask people about how they think others would respond to sanctioning efforts. Obviously, individuals who are afraid of retaliation are less likely to punish. But the relational theory points to the importance of support from others (not just potential retaliation by the deviant). That is, how do people think others in the neighborhood will respond to their sanctioning activity? Do they think that if they take action against bad behavior, neighbors will respond positively? Or do they think that they will be abandoned to whatever negative fate might befall them? Do they expect that if they intervene to chastise neighborhood teenagers, they will be viewed positively by other neighborhood residents? Or do they fear that they will be left to act on their own without support? To my knowledge such questions have not been asked systematically. Because the theory suggests that people consider what will happen to them if they sanction, it would make sense to ask them about their expectations.

We might also consider how people use others' characteristics as clues about the extent to which they would support sanctioning. Consider race, for example. Race is a highly salient characteristic in American society. Social psychological research suggests that people (of all races) use race as an indicator of competence and prosociality (Ridgeway 2001; Webster and Driskell 1978). They expect whites to be more competent and group-oriented and blacks to be less so. Thus if individuals are looking around their neighborhood and trying to anticipate how others are likely to react to their sanctioning efforts, they might expect whites to respond more positively than blacks. Their expectations may not be correct, but in the absence of other information, people may make this default assumption.

People might make similar assumptions about poverty. But interestingly, while poverty often sends a negative message about the poor person, in some situations it may not. Like race, income may be seen as an indicator of an individual's competence and prosociality. People are likely to assume that the wealthy are superior to the poor. But people may not make this assumption if they can attribute poverty to causes other than the individual's failings. For example, in rural areas, people may attribute poverty to the federal government and environmentalists whom they see as reducing local job opportunities. In such situations, low pay or joblessness does not necessarily imply anything negative about the individual. We might expect, therefore, that metanorm and norm enforcement will be stronger in poor rural communities than in poor urban neighborhoods.

People might also use the physical characteristics of a neighborhood as a source of information about the extent to which residents care about their community. One might well assume that if there are broken windows, graffiti, and so forth, residents are unlikely to intervene or to support control efforts that benefit the community. (For a related argument, see Kelling and Coles 1996; Wilson and Kelling 1982; and Zimbardo 2008.) Such perceptions not only encourage criminals; they also discourage individuals from taking action against crime.

Criminologists recognize that they have been more successful at identifying correlates of crime than the mechanisms responsible for them. As Sampson (2000) says, "[M]ost criminological theory is static in logic and handicapped by a focus on (allegedly) fixed explanatory categories, thereby failing to address the processes and dynamics leading to criminal events. The most important thing about crime that we do not know, in other words, concerns its causal social processes" (p. 711). The relational theory of norms provides insight into mechanisms that underlie the informal control of crime. By illuminating these processes, it suggests further questions we could be asking and data we could be seeking.

Metanorm Expectations: Explaining the Enforcement of International Human Rights Norms

Earlier in this book, I described Chilean dictator Pinochet's support for the anti-torture convention (Chapter 3). Because Pinochet was an abusive ruler responsible for the torture and deaths of many, his support of such norm enforcement efforts is particularly puzzling. The question of why nations enforce international human rights norms is broader, however, than simply understanding Pinochet. There have been a number of attempts to enforce human rights norms, with many countries committing to do so.

A recent, significant effort is the International Criminal Court (ICC). The ICC is a remarkable institution with jurisdiction over a number of serious human rights violations, including genocide, crimes against humanity, and war crimes. The statute authorizing the ICC was adopted in 1998. Observers expected that it would take a long time to accumulate the number of commitments necessary, but by April 2002, sixty states had ratified, and in July of that year, the Court was formed.

The quick creation of the ICC was surprising to many. Commitment to the ICC was potentially costly. A nation that committed, for example, gave foreign bodies jurisdiction over its citizens and territory. Given such costs, why did countries commit?

The theory described in this book suggests that metanorms and relations between actors were key. Political scientists Jay Goodliffe, Darren Hawkins, Dan Nielson, and I worked together to explore this possibility. The results of our study are reported in Goodliffe et al. (2008). Here I describe the study and highlight some of our findings.

As with the previous illustrations, before discussing the application of the theory, I consider whether the international arena is an appropriate setting. Consistent with the theoretical scope conditions, nations share a world in which human rights abuses occur. These nations interact with each other and they interact over time. Further, they know (or have a pretty good idea) that abuses have occurred and by whom. And they have information about other countries' sanctioning efforts. Thus the international human rights arena is an appropriate context in which to apply the relational theory of norms.

Application of the Theory

The theory seeks to explain norm enforcement. Commitment to the International Criminal Court can be conceptualized as an instance of such enforcement. When countries ratify the ICC, they are, in effect, committing to an enforcement institution—committing to the enforcement of international human rights norms. Countries can enforce norms individually. They can refuse to trade with a country. They can unilaterally send soldiers. But they can also delegate authority to an agent to carry out the enforcement (Hawkins 2004). The ICC is such an agent. Thus, commitment to the ICC represents commitment to enforcing human rights norms.

What does the relational theory of norms suggest about why nations would commit to the ICC? A key insight of the theory is that when actors make sanctioning decisions, they consider the likely reactions of others.

Nations have clues about these potential reactions. One clue is what other countries are doing (see Chapter 5). If other countries follow human rights norms and treat their citizens well, that is evidence that they value human rights and would react positively to those who punish violators. Arguably, countries' sanctioning actions provide another indication that they disapprove of human rights abuses and that they would react favorably to those who punish such bad behavior. If so, then the number of countries that have committed to the International Criminal Court affects a nation's expectation of how it will be treated if it commits.

But not everyone's commitment matters equally. Nations care more about the potential reactions of countries on which they are dependent.[1]

When a nation is dependent on others that have committed to the ICC, it cares about maintaining relations with those countries and about evoking positive rather than negative reactions. It therefore is more likely to commit itself. When it is dependent on those who have not committed, it is less likely to commit. Accordingly, the higher the proportion of a country's network that has committed to the ICC, the more likely it is to also commit. Dependence on others that have committed to the ICC can be seen as an indicator of metanorms.

Countries may depend on each other for a variety of goods—natural resources, political support, people, and so forth. It is difficult to know which domains matter the most. Given this difficulty, we decided to look at multiple domains. We measured dependence by using an index that incorporated security alliances, trade relations, and shared membership in international organizations. Security alliances help countries protect themselves. Trade relations provide goods and income. Membership in international organizations provides opportunities to gain support for achieving a variety of policy goals. Each of these domains captures a potentially valued component of relationships between countries.

Metanorms are an abstract concept. In order to measure them, we identified the countries in each nation's network and measured the level of dependence between them. We calculated the proportion of those countries that had committed to the ICC each year. Based on the theory, we expected this measure to have a positive effect on the individual nation's commitment.

Alternative Explanations

In addition to applying the relational theory of norms, we tested alternative explanations suggested by the international relations literature. Consistent with the behavior consequences approach, this literature suggests that a nation will join an international institution when doing so provides some benefit to it (Abbott and Snidal 2000; Koremenos et al. 2001). For example, when new democracies are vulnerable and unstable, they may commit to an international institution in order to lock in democratic principles within the country (Moravcsik 2000). Similarly, the less costly it is for a nation to join an institution, the more likely it is to do so. These costs may vary for different countries (Goodliffe and Hawkins 2006). Those that experience the lowest costs are most likely to commit. This approach would suggest that the costs and benefits a country experiences will affect whether or not it commits to the ICC.

Consistent with the meanings approach, some international relations scholars criticize the behavior consequences logic, pointing out that countries often do things that do not increase their welfare. These scholars argue that nations care not only about consequences but also about identity and legitimacy. Countries join an international institution when doing so seems appropriate or consistent with its identity (Finnemore and Sikkink 1998; Meyer et al. 1997). On this view, when many countries in the world or in a particular region have committed to an international institution, others are more likely to do so as well (see, for example, Cole 2005). Individual nations will follow the majority because majority behavior becomes taken for granted—it is simply what countries do. In the ICC context, the meanings approach suggests that the more countries in a region (or around the world) that have committed, the more likely any individual nation in that region is to commit as well.

Results

Our empirical analyses (described in Goodliffe et al. 2008) provide support for the relational theory of norms. The findings show that the two strongest predictors of commitment to the ICC were metanorms and sanctioning costs. Thus it appears that a particular consequence (the cost of sanctioning) in conjunction with social considerations (relations with countries that had committed to the ICC) drove countries' commitment decisions.

Another consequentialist variable, the benefits of commitment, did not have an effect. Thus the support for the consequentialist approach was mixed.

There also was little support for the meanings approach. The number of countries in a region that had committed had an effect—but only when metanorms were not included. When metanorms were added to the analyses, the effect of prior commitment by countries in a region disappeared.

The results of this study are consistent with the relational theory of norms. The findings show that countries considered more than just the costs and benefits of committing to the ICC. An important part of the reason that nations committed was their relations with other countries and the likely reactions of their interaction partners. In other words, social relations, and metanorms in particular, mattered.

Discussion

In this chapter, I have provided three illustrations of how the relational theory of norm enforcement might be applied to address substantive questions. My intent here is not to present full-blown empirical analyses, but, rather, to provide some illustrative examples of ways in which the relational theory of norms might be useful outside the lab. These examples suggest that the norms theory presented in this book is not only predictive in the lab but also has the potential to explain social phenomena in the field.

The theory may have implications for a range of substantive domains other than the three explored here. Scholars interested in education have found that achievement varies across schools and across subgroups within schools. An individual's success is a function not only of his own personal characteristics, but also of his social context. Norms theory provides a tool for identifying components of that social context that might matter. Health researchers find that physician practices vary across geographic region. The reasons for this are unclear. Might norms be a part of the explanation? Political scientists study state legitimacy. What does it mean to be legitimate, and what is it that makes one regime more legitimate than another? Might it be helpful to conceptualize legitimacy as a norm—a norm that says that people ought to support the government? Online exchange systems rely on information and sanctioning to reduce bad behavior. Might greater understanding of enforcement contribute to more effective designs of such systems? Members of the same ethnic groups tend to be more successful at working together to provide public goods than members of different ethnic groups. Might norms be part of the reason? (Habyarimana, Humphreys, Posner, and Weinstein 2007 provide evidence that the answer is yes.)

Norms are relevant in many areas of social life. The fact that interdependence and metanorms matter for norm enforcement suggests that we ought to pay close attention to the structure of relationships. Changes in social relations affect norms and the behaviors they regulate. Frequently such considerations remain in the background, however. Policy makers debate the relative utility of government intervention and market incentives. They argue about the precise form such interventions and incentive structures should take. When we use government regulations or market incentives to solve social problems, those efforts may or may not produce the desired results. But they also may or may not affect the structure of social relations. If social relations affect norms, and if norms matter, then we ought to consider how policy interventions will affect them. In the next chapter, I describe one approach to thinking about the connection between norms and governments and markets.

7 Norms, Laws, and Markets

Implications for Policy

I N 1955, CONGRESS EXTENDED THE SOCIAL SECURITY ACT TO apply to self-employed farmers—including the Amish. While the Amish had no objection to paying taxes, they resented being forced to participate in a social insurance scheme. They neither wanted to pay into such a scheme nor accept the benefits. Amish farmer Valentine Byler expressed his disapproval by refusing to pay. In response, the IRS took away his plough horses while he was working in his fields. The outcry led the government to relent—releasing the Amish from paying into Social Security (Igou 2007; Ferrara 1993).

The Amish not only object to insurance schemes run by the government; they also refuse other kinds of benefits that are provided through the market. They avoid, for example, many products that are available to help make farming less labor-intensive. They prefer horse-drawn ploughs over tractors. They do not own telephones. They do not drive cars.[1] Why do they choose a way of life that involves such hard work? Do they know something that we do not?

The Amish see ties to governments and markets as a potential threat. If they paid into Social Security, they might also be tempted to take benefits from it. But such behavior would weaken the interdependence of family and community members, reducing the ability of the Amish to maintain their way of life. According to Mennonite Bishop Jesse Neuenschwander, who testified before Congress, "Our greatest problem is when our people become recipients of Social Security benefits, rather than allow the church to care for their own" (quoted in Glenn 2001). If tractors, cars, and farming equipment were permissible, a single individual could complete tasks that, without these tools, would require the coordinated physical labor of community members. By connecting economically with the outside world, community members would be disconnecting from each other. They would be less interdependent. Informal controls would weaken. The injunction to "come out from among them and be ye separate" (2 Corinthians 6:17) has a practical rationale.

There is a lot of debate about the appropriate role of governments and markets in addressing social problems. Much of it focuses on whether government penalties or market incentives will be most effective and efficient at producing the desired results. This book points to norms as an additional source of solutions. But, as the Amish example attests, neither governments, nor markets, nor community norms exist in a vacuum. If norms are a potential solution to problems, then we need to understand their connection to other institutions. If we create legal penalties or market incentives, we want them to be effective at producing the desired results. It is likely, however, that such interventions will also have effects on norms. That is, markets and government regulations may have direct effects on problematic behavior. But they can also have indirect effects through their impacts on communities and the informal controls exercised within them. The Amish appear to be sensitive to these effects. But our policy debates often say little about them. For interventions to be effective, we might be wise to consider not only the direct effects of governments and markets on behavior, but also their unintended consequences. One such consequence may be a weakening of social relationships and, in turn, the enforcement of norms. Paradoxically, legal actions meant to increase social order could actually have the opposite effect.

Law and Norms

The relationship between law and norms is complex. Many researchers have explored pieces of the connections between them. Here I focus on one type of connection suggested by the relational theory of norm enforcement. That is, I examine how law might affect social relations—in particular, interdependence.

Sometimes law affects social relations explicitly. State-sanctioned marriage, for example, supports some relationships over others. Laws governing corporations privilege certain kinds of organization. But law also has less obvious effects. Even when it does not explicitly regulate relationships, it can change them nonetheless. Scholars have debated these effects for centuries.

Some suggest that the state weakens social relationships. Anarchists, in particular, are known for making these criticisms. Kropotkin argued that "there is an inverse correlation between [society and the state]: the strength of one is the weakness of the other. If we want to strengthen society, we must weaken the state" (quoted in Ward 1973, 250). Expressing a similar view, legal scholar Jhering said that "[t]he progress of law consists in the destruction of every natural tie, in a continued process of separation and isolation" (quoted in Diamond 1971, 52).

The reasons given for these negative effects of government are varied. In general, they suggest that law changes individuals—crowding out prosocial motivations so that people no longer desire to help others.

Some argue that when people are regulated by the legal system, they come to see each other as self-interested and as needing to be controlled. Trust declines as a result (Taylor 1987; see also Gellner 1988). Thus when the IRS publicizes increased efforts to catch tax cheaters and larger penalties for violations, it makes people think that cheating is common. This belief reduces commitment to paying taxes. In turn, people increase the deductions that they take (Sheffrin and Triest 1992).

Others argue that because law mediates relationships between individuals, it produces a weakened sense of duty for others (Taylor 1987). People may feel that paying taxes takes care of any responsibility that they have. They do not have to cooperate directly with others and can instead do what they please. Individuals do not have to worry about giving to the poor if they think that government is providing. They do not have to worry about other people's children if public schools are doing the job. One reformer says, "As each individual abandons himself to the solicitous aid of the State, so, and still more, he abandons to it the fate of his fellow-citizens. This weakens sympathy and renders mutual assistance inactive" (Humboldt [1854] 1969, quoted in Taylor 1987, 174).

While some scholars suggest that law weakens community, others argue that it is essential for the development and maintenance of social relationships. Hobbes ([1651] 1958) provides the classic statement of this view:

> During the time men live without a common power to keep them all in awe, they are in that condition which is called war, and such a war as is of every man against every man. . . . [T]he bonds of words are too weak to bridle mans ambition, avarice and other passions without the fear of some coercive power. . . . [C]ovenants without the sword are but words of no strength to secure a man at all. (pp. 89, 109, 106)

According to Hobbes, without law people cannot form productive relationships.

More recently, scholars have suggested that law "may protect a relationship against the worst of all risks it might entail, thereby enabling the parties to cooperate on more risky matters. . . . [T]he threat of sanctions to protect each makes all better off. . . . [W]e have less reason to be defensive and we engage in productive investments and beneficial exchanges" (Hardin 1996, 32). The existence (and therefore the threat) of legal sanctions reduces the risk of interaction—thereby facilitating the development and maintenance of productive social relationships. Legal recourse may strengthen people's confidence that others will comply with group rules, making commitments within the group more likely (Hardin 1996; Schwartz and Miller 1964).

Some scholars have recognized that law may have both effects—strengthening or weakening social relations—depending on how it is designed. Eric Posner (1996a) provides an analysis that is particularly useful given the focus of this book. Rather than emphasizing internal motivation, he looks at the effects of different types of law on groups. He identifies two types as important—category-based and group-based.

Category-based laws provide benefits to categories of people— women, minorities, the elderly, children, workers, and so forth. Employment laws, for example, provide protections to workers without regard to their group memberships. Laws against discrimination based on sex or race protect women and minorities.

Group-based laws, by contrast, provide benefits to members of groups like unions or families. Labor law assists workers who belong to a union rather than workers in general. Laws that protect spouses from testifying against each other apply only to couples.

Posner argues that when a law provides benefits to an entire category of people, it weakens groups. This is because individuals can get benefits from the government without help from anybody else. They are no longer dependent on the group for those benefits. Employment laws that protect the rights of workers, for example, reduce the need for unions.

When law benefits groups, however, then those groups have even greater ability to serve their members, and individuals are dependent on the group for those benefits. Labor laws that give unions the ability to bargain for their members strengthen unions. Posner argues that category-based laws weaken social groups, while group-based laws strengthen them.

More generally, Posner's argument suggests that when law provides a substitute source of goods, it weakens groups. In this chapter I focus on the effects that law has on social relationships (and by extension on norms) when it provides a substitute source of control.

The Effect of Law on Interdependence

For several years, I lived in the downtown barrio in Tucson, Arizona. The neighborhood consisted of Mexican families who had been in the area for many years, low-income creative types from the local music scene, students seeking cheap rent, and some upscale homes and architect offices. One of these offices was around the corner from me. In the other direction was a neighbor I knew from his noisy truck running outside my window as he went to the drive-through liquor store down the block.

One day I came home to learn that someone had broken into the architect's office and had stolen a computer. Like many crooks, the thief was not very clever. In the process of stealing the computer, he had cut himself. As he carried the computer home, he left a trail of blood that led the police to his—my truck-driving neighbor's—front door.

The architect did what I would have done. He called the police. But he had a choice. He could also have followed the trail of blood himself. Such a choice would have been risky, however. He had no idea what craziness he might find at the other end. So he did what many of us do: He turned to the law.

When others engage in damaging behavior, we have two choices. We can try to address the problem ourselves. We can enforce norms and bear all of the associated costs and risks. Or, if the behavior is regulated by government, we can turn to the legal system that is supported by taxes. Norms are rules that are socially enforced. Laws are rules enforced by government. When a rule can be enforced both socially and by the legal system, then individuals can choose how they wish to address violations.

The legal institution is an agent of the group. It punishes those who break the rules. Its expenses are paid, at least to some extent, through taxes imposed on all group members.

A legal system is stronger when it has more financial resources—when taxes bring in a lot of money. As its resources increase, it is better able to cover its expenses. In turn, it can impose lower costs on individual users. In a state with a strong legal institution, for example, people using the courts are unlikely to have to pay personally for the services of a judge, the upkeep of the courts, or the maintenance of prisoners. In some rural Indian communities, women take lunch to family members serving time in the local jail. They, rather than the government, are responsible for prison food. We would not see this behavior in a society with a strong tax base and legal institution. Or consider the 911 emergency telephone system: Maintaining the 911 system costs money, but when it is in place, it is easier for individuals to report a crime or other emergency. Similarly, anonymous hotlines lower the costs to individuals of reporting child abuse.

Group members activate legal sanctions when they make demands on the government—call the police, file a court case, and so forth.[2] Because a legal system with more resources can pass fewer costs on to users (who therefore have less additional expense on top of their existing taxes), individuals are more likely to take advantage of it. Filing a lawsuit is less appealing if the plaintiff has to pay all attorney fees than if he has a state-provided lawyer. Residents are more likely to report a crime if they can call 911 than if they have to go to the local precinct and complete lots of paperwork. In general, people are more likely to turn to the legal system (call the police, file a lawsuit, and so forth) when doing so is easy and cheap.

Of course, within a particular society there may be variation in the costs of different kinds of legal action. For example, it is less personally costly to make a phone call than to file a lawsuit. Here, however, I focus on a more general measure of costs that can be compared across societies or across different time periods in the same society. Any legal system can be conceptualized as having an overall strength even though different kinds of complaints might be associated with varying degrees of state involvement. In general, legal systems will be stronger when they have more money.

Whereas the strength of the legal institution varies with its financial resources, the strength of a group varies with its social resources—the extent to which individuals rely upon each other to attain valued ends. In other words, groups are stronger when members are interdependent. And, as shown in earlier chapters, interdependence increases the enforcement of group norms.

Group members enforce norms when they personally punish deviant behavior. They might criticize the deviant, confront him, avoid contact

with him, and so forth. Whereas the costs of sanctioning legally are sub-
sidized partially by taxes, the costs of punishing normatively are born
fully by individuals.

Like legal sanctioning, the cost of imposing normative sanctions
varies. It is scarier to confront a murdering drug dealer than to correct
a child's table manners. Here, again, I am not focusing on distinctions
between the seriousness of behavior consequences, but on the general,
structural distinctions between legal and normative sanctions and the
ways in which their costs are allocated.

All else being equal, individuals bear higher costs if they impose
sanctions themselves than if they turn to the legal system. This is because
they are paying not only taxes, but also the personal expense of normative sanctioning. This assertion obviously ignores the complexity of fully
determining the relative costs of norms and law. Behaviors that occur
within a family, for example, are more easily observed by parents and
siblings than by the government. If the state tried to monitor such behavior, it would be very expensive. Here, I suggest that if we control for
these other sources of expense, it will be more appealing for individuals
to use the legal system than to take action informally. This is because
many of the costs of using the law are shared with others through the tax
system. The personal costs of normative sanctioning compared with the
shared costs of legal sanctioning create an incentive for people to turn to
the law. Just like the architect around the corner, many of us would prefer not to bear the risks ourselves.

How do people respond to community members who punish antisocial behavior? The relational theory of norm enforcement suggests that
people will react more positively to those who sanction normatively
than to those who use the legal system—at least when the legal system is
strong and relatively inexpensive to access. This is because, as seen in
Chapter 4, metanorm enforcers pay attention to the personal costs that
sanctioners experience. In particular, they are sensitive to giving support proportional to the sanctioner's need. Giving too much is unnecessary to sustain the relationship and is unlikely to be repaid fully. But
giving too little will not ensure the continuation of the relationship and

future reciprocal help. Thus the higher the sanctioner's cost, the more others are likely to give in support. To the extent that the expenses of legal sanctioning are covered through taxes rather than by the individual user, sanctioners will experience lower personal costs and therefore require less in the way of rewards. For this reason, the more that people in a group turn to personally inexpensive legal sanctions rather than rely on normative punishment, the less social support will be given to sanctioners overall.

This decrease in reward levels leads to a weaker, less cohesive community. Individuals value relationships that are rewarding and that have some degree of stability. People act under conditions of uncertainty when they choose to sanction in a way that is personally costly. They hope that they will be rewarded for their action, but are not necessarily sure that they will be. Similarly, individuals who reward sanctioners lose in the short run but hope for a continued relationship (and reciprocal rewards) in the future. For both sanctioners and other community members, if they take the risk, incur the costs, and are rewarded for doing so, then they will begin to have greater confidence in others. If they do not make such attempts, or if their actions are not reciprocated, then their confidence will remain low and their interactions will be less productive. For individuals who prefer certainty, uncertain and unproductive relationships are less valuable.[3] And when relationships are not valued, people have little reason to turn to each other. Interdependence is low.

Thus a strong legal system and the availability of personally inexpensive legal sanctioning lead to increased use of law. This results in lower levels of social support and mutual rewarding within the community. People become less interdependent. In turn, they are less likely to enforce metanorms and norms. In other words, a strong legal institution weakens communities and their ability to enforce norms by providing an alternative to informal controls. This alternative reduces people's dependence on each other. If this theory is right, law does not simply emerge in response to weaker normative controls, as is often suggested. It may also actually weaken those controls.

Experiment 9: Legal and Normative Controls

I tested these predictions using a variant of the Metanorms Game. In the standard Metanorms Game, individuals could choose to punish theft and to react to the sanctioning decisions of others. In this experiment, subjects could punish theft in one of two ways. They could choose to sanction normatively, just as they did in the other studies. But they also could choose to sanction legally. And, of course, they could decide not to punish at all. As in the earlier experiments, they could use opportunities for exchange to express approval or disapproval of sanctioning decisions.

I manipulated two experimental conditions—interdependence and the strength of the legal system (Table 7.1). I manipulated interdependence in the same way as I did in the earlier Metanorms Game experi-

TABLE 7.1 Experiment 9 conditions

	Weak Legal System	*Strong Legal System*
Low Interdependence	1:1 Low Tax High Cost	1:1 High Tax Low Cost
High Interdependence	1:3 Low Tax High Cost	1:3 High Tax Low Cost

SOURCE: Based on research published in "Community and the State: The Relationship Between Normative and Legal Controls." *European Sociological Review* 16(3): 225–43.
NOTE: I ran ten groups of four in each condition for a total of forty groups.

ments, varying the value of points received from others relative to the subject's own.

Unlike those experiments, this one also manipulated the strength of the legal system. Strength of the legal system is defined in terms of its financial resources. I manipulated it by varying the amount of tax that was collected to support the legal agent (the computer) and the related personal costs of using legal sanctions. In the weak law condition, subjects had to pay 10 points (in addition to their taxes) if they chose to sanction legally. In the strong law condition they paid nothing other than their taxes. In both conditions, it cost 10 points to sanction normatively.

I was interested in how the experimental conditions affected the frequency with which subjects chose to sanction legally. In turn, I expected that frequent legal sanctions would lead to lower levels of support for sanctioners generally. I therefore measured the mean rewards given to those who engaged in any kind of sanctioning (normative or legal). Finally, I measured the value that subjects placed on their relationships at the end of the experiment. The more that subjects valued their relationships, the more interdependent the group.

The results show that when the legal institution was stronger (and cheaper for individuals to use), people were more likely to turn to it for help. Use of the law was higher when the legal system was strong (Table 7.2 and Model 1 in Table 7.3).

In turn, people gave smaller rewards. In interdependent groups, rewards were larger when the legal system was weak (and legal sanctioning was costly) than when it was strong (and legal sanctioning was free). As the number of legal sanctions in a group increased, people gave less support to sanctioners (Table 7.2 and Model 2 in Table 7.3). Overall reward levels within the group declined.

As predicted, this reduction in support lowered the value that people placed on their relationships with their fellow group members. Rewards for sanctioners affected the value that participants placed on their relationships at the end of the experiment (Model 3 in Table 7.3).

The results are consistent with the argument that when the legal system provides an alternative, less personally costly source of control, people

TABLE 7.2 Mean measures across interdependence and legal system conditions

		Weak Legal System		Strong Legal System	
		Mean	SD	Mean	SD
Low Interdependence	Legal Sanctions	.398	(.177)	.691	(.198)
	Rewards for Sanctioning	2.57	(1.86)	2.19	(1.51)
	Value of Relations	4.87	(.792)	4.47	(1.06)
High Interdependence	Legal Sanctions	.268	(.156)	.689	(.174)
	Rewards for Sanctioning	9.62	(2.63)	6.66	(1.54)
	Value of Relations	5.60	(.866)	5.63	(.526)

NOTE: $N=10$ in each condition.

TABLE 7.3 OLS regression explaining legal sanctioning, rewards, and the value of relationships

	Legal Sanctioning		Rewards for Sanctioning		Value of Relationships	
	Model 1		Model 2		Model 3	
Intercept	.298***	(.0560)	3.74***	(.775)	4.45***	(.302)
Interdependence	−.0295	(.0793)	6.93***	(.822)	−.407	(.589)
Strength Legal System	.393***	(.0793)	1.16	(1.07)	−.338	(.351)
Interdependence × Strength Legal System	.0273	(.112)	−2.47*	(1.16)	.841	(.524)
Legal Sanctions	——		− 3.92*	(1.73)	——	
Rewards for Sanctioning	——		——		.162*	(.0673)
R-Square	.59		.77		.38	

NOTE: Standard errors are in parentheses.
$N=40$.
*$p<.05$, **$p<.001$, ***$p<.0001$ (two-tailed tests)

turn to it rather than take action themselves. In turn, they interact less. The value they place on their relationships diminishes; interdependence declines. In sum, a strong legal system weakens social relations. We would therefore expect (as demonstrated by the other experiments described in this book) that there will be less norm enforcement—fewer efforts by individuals to punish deviance.

Markets and Norms

The experimental results are consistent with the theory that when law provides a substitute source of valued goods, it weakens social relations, and in turn, the informal enforcement of norms. Just as law may change the structure of social relations, so too may markets. Many argue that free markets and the voluntary actions of citizens are the solution to a range of problems, including costly health care, inadequate pensions, poor education outcomes, and so forth. According to these analyses, limited government must be accompanied by strong markets. Solutions to problems should be informal, not mandated by a central authority. But this view implies that strong markets can exist simultaneously with citizens who enforce and comply with prosocial norms. (For a discussion of this issue, see Sacks 1999 with related commentaries by Barry, Davidson, and Novak.) Is this possible?

Scholars disagree over the effects that markets have (Fourcade and Healy 2007; Hirschman 1982). Some argue that markets strengthen social relationships. People involved in economic transactions must be able to trust each other. They also care about their reputations. Market economies therefore increase both trust and trustworthiness. Consistent with this view, research shows that transactions under conditions of uncertainty increase trust—thereby strengthening the relationships between those involved in the exchange (Henrich et al. 2004; Kollock 1994; Yamagishi, Cook, and Watabe 1998).

Other advocates argue that markets increase wealth and that wealth, in turn, makes people more cooperative. In his *Theory of Moral Sentiments*, Adam Smith says: "Before we can feel much for others, we must in some measure be at ease ourselves. If our own misery pinches us very severely, we have no leisure to attend to that of our neighbors" (Friedman 2005, 49–50; see also Frey and Stutzer 2002). If hardship reduces the likelihood that an individual will help another, then well-being ought to increase that likelihood. A contemporary of Smith's, John Millar, makes just such an argument: "According as men have been successful in these great improvements, and find less difficulty in the attainment of bare necessaries . . . men, being less oppressed with their own wants, are more at liberty to cultivate . . . feelings of humanity . . ." (Millar 1771 quoted in Meek 1976, 163). Recent versions of this argument suggest that markets provide individuals with resources—including more time and money. People who feel wealthy can use these resources to invest in their communities—in relationships, in parks, and in a variety of public goods (Friedman 2005, 12).[4] Markets improve individual well-being, and individual well-being translates into stronger communities. To the extent that markets have this effect, the relational theory suggests that they ought to produce stronger norms.

Whereas some researchers suggest that markets strengthen relationships and cooperative behavior, others argue that they have the opposite effect. They provide evidence that capitalism weakens social relationships (Bourdieu 2000; Polanyi 1944). For example, markets destroy relationships when they encourage mobility (Elster 1989, 284–85). This can happen when promotions require moves to new companies or cities. It can also occur when market forces lead to job losses. When companies seeking to maximize profits close down a factory, employees must move on. Families break down. Marriage declines (Sweeney 2002; Wilson 1987). Relationships are disrupted. Similarly, economic booms can lead to social dislocation. In turn, when communities decline, they are less able to solve collective problems.

The relational theory of norms suggests that, like law, markets will weaken groups when they offer members alternative, cheaper sources of valued goods. When they do so, they reduce peoples' dependence on other individuals in their group. People do not need to be as concerned about others' opinions. In turn, we would expect norm enforcement to decline.

The theory presented in this book suggests that part of the effect of laws and markets on norms depends on whether and how they affect the structure of social relations. Do they complement what groups already do (for example, providing services that groups are unable to provide) or do they displace groups? When governments or markets create substitutes for what is successfully provided informally (and do so at a lower cost to the individual), group members will begin to turn to those sources rather than to each other. Rewarding interactions will decline. People will be less interdependent. They will be less likely to sanction deviance. Norms will become weaker.

Policy As If Social Relations Matter

What are the implications of norms for social policy? Some discussions recognize, to a degree, the importance of relationships. They acknowledge, for example, the contribution of social capital to a range of desirable outcomes. Despite this recognition, the relative strengths of government and market solutions continue to dominate public discourse. We do not pay much attention to the ways in which these solutions affect relationships and the norms they support. How would we think about public policy if we saw people not just as atomistic individuals, but also as social beings?

I illustrate a possibility by considering education. In the United States, we have outstanding, good, merely adequate, and outright failing schools. We regularly hear calls for reform. The challenge is to improve education outcomes, to move our failing schools to acceptability, and to move our acceptable or even good schools to excellence. Two solutions dominate public discourse on the issue.

The first relies on government-mandated standards, tests, and penalties for failure. In 2001, the U.S. Congress passed the No Child Left Behind Act. Under the terms of the statute, states must develop standards that students are expected to meet. If schools fail to make adequate yearly progress toward meeting those standards, they need to provide their students with tutoring or the opportunity to transfer to another school. If school test scores remain low, the school may be subject to restructuring by the state.

The perception driving this strategy is that poor learning outcomes are caused by schools and teachers failing to set and uphold high standards. Schools are hiring unqualified teachers, or teachers are not working hard enough, or teachers just do not have sufficiently high expectations.

The No Child Left Behind solution to the problem is to hold schools and teachers accountable for failure. If government raises the bar, and imposes consequences for failure to meet that bar, then teachers will do a better job and students will succeed.

Market advocates also think that schools and teachers are not doing a good enough job. But they suggest a different solution. They argue that if market mechanisms are allowed to operate—through school choice, vouchers, charter schools, and so forth—schools and teachers will want to do better. They will be motivated to improve in order to attract students and to keep their jobs. If students can vote with their feet, they will leave and go to the better schools. Just as consumers seek and buy superior products, students will seek superior schools. Subject to such market pressures, schools will develop positive attributes. Student learning will improve as a result.

The market solution rewards schools and teachers for success. If they do a good job, they will attract students and resources. If they do not, they will fail.

Each of these approaches has something to recommend it. Standards are arguably a good thing. The disciplinary power of the market is widely recognized.

Yet, neither of these approaches is a perfect solution. Both have weaknesses that undermine their potential positive effects. For example, both are vulnerable to teacher cheating. They provide incentives not only for teachers to *do* a better job, but also for them to *look* like they are doing a better job (Levitt and Dubner 2006).

The relational theory of norms highlights another weakness. Both government and market approaches see the challenge of improving student learning as an individual-level issue. Accordingly, the way to address the problem is to change the incentives—either by providing penalties for doing poorly or rewards for doing well. But neither of these approaches recognizes that both students and teachers are social beings influenced by their social surroundings. Neither recognizes the power of norms.

There is good evidence that norms matter in the education context. Many researchers have documented the importance of peers for educational outcomes. Just as mom and dad thought, it matters who your friends are. Children with the same background learn more or less depending on their peers (Coleman 1966). Teenagers who go to schools where many of the students are in academic tracks do better than those who attend schools where few are in such tracks (Bryk, Lee, and Smith 1990). Those who have high-achieving friends do better than those with low-achieving friends (Epstein 1983). Those who go to school with middle-class youth learn more than those who attend with poor students (Kahlenberg 2001). Those who have delinquent friends are more likely to be delinquent than those who have well-behaved peers (Haynie 2001).

Very early on, American children form groups distinct from adults. As early as preschool, children conspire with each other to circumvent adult rules (Corsaro 1985). It just gets worse as they get older. Adolescents and teenagers are notoriously concerned with popularity (Coleman 1961; Cusick 1973; Harris 1999). They want friends of the same sex and approval of the opposite sex. Popularity is based on what peers think, not what teachers or parents want.

Because peers are so important for teens, peers influence behavior both in and out of school. Teenagers do not wear the clothes their teachers wear; they wear styles peers approve. They do not talk like their teachers; they talk like their friends. They do not do what their teachers do for fun; they do what their friends do. And they do not learn what teachers know; they learn what their peers think it is important to know—what music to listen to, what to wear, and what to do on the weekend.

Researchers report numerous examples of peer influence in the educational context. In the 1980s, college student Jay McLeod started a summer job as a youth counselor in a low-income public housing development. After a few years, he began talking to these children's older siblings—their teenage role models. His conversations were the basis of his senior thesis, which he later published as a book. McLeod (1995, 119) describes the culture of the "hallway hangers"):

JINKS: I'd say everyone more or less has the same attitudes towards school: fuck it. Except the bookworms—people who don't just hang around outside and drink, get high, who sit at home—they're the ones who get an education.

JM: And they just decide for themselves?

JINKS: Yup.

JM: So why don't more people decide that way?

JINKS: Y'know what it is Jay? We all don't break away because we're too tight. Our friends are important to us. Fuck it. If we can't make it together, fuck it. Fuck it all.

These dynamics occur not just among lower-class youth but also in middle-class schools, which are by all accounts functioning (Cusick 1973, 67). In one such high school, students told a researcher:

"The worst thing that can happen is that you have to walk around the halls alone."
"What about the cafeteria?"
"Oh, that's even worse. Kids would rather not eat than eat alone."
After that, the researcher frequently asked students "What would you rather do, flunk a test or eat alone in the cafeteria?"
The answer: "Flunk a test!"

The stories these students tell are consistent with large-scale studies. Peer influence, it seems, is crucial for student motivation to work and for the ability of teachers to set high expectations. Social pressure can be a positive for those who are fortunate enough to have peers who value education and understand the work required. But peer pressure does not work so well for students whose peers come from homes where parents do not mind if their children get Cs or Ds, where people do not understand that a community college is different from the state university or an elite private college, and where students do not recognize the effort required to develop skills. In these settings, peers may enforce norms that do not encourage high levels of achievement.

These social pressures matter. Students care more about the opinions of their friends than their teachers. This is not surprising. Peer punishments can be severe and students have to deal with those peers every day. Students eat lunch with each other, typically with those of the same age; teachers eat lunch in the staff room. Students share public restrooms; teachers have access to their own. Students have lockers in the hallway; teachers keep their coats in the teachers' lounge. Students move from class to class; teachers stay in their rooms.

In this environment, it makes sense that peers, not teachers, determine whether a student has a good day or a bad day. Teachers may stand in front of classes, or even meet with students after school, but they are not an integral part of a student's social network. Because students interact so much with peers, those peers, more than teachers, are in a position to make life miserable. This means that students are more dependent on their peers for approval than they are on their teachers. They have to anticipate what their friends and acquaintances (not just their teachers) will approve.

There are other reasons for students not to value teachers. Teachers in the United States do not control access to jobs. They control grades, but high school grades have little relation to success in the job market. Further, given the emphasis on aptitude (as measured by SAT results) rather than knowledge and skills, students do not actually have to have learned much to get into college. In this environment, teacher approval does not provide motivation for students to want to achieve and to enforce pro-education norms.

These facts have implications for learning. When students enforce norms that undermine learning, or simply fail to enforce norms that encourage it, little learning is likely to occur. As any teacher knows, his power in the classroom is limited by the ability and motivation of students to rebel (McFarland 2001).

Just as students are affected by their social environment, so too are teachers. Unlike students, however, they tend to be isolated from their peers. American teachers teach alone. On busy days, there may be few opportunities for them to interact with each other. School infrastructure often does not encourage teachers to work together. The relational theory of norms suggests that, given this lack of interaction, pro-education norms among teachers are likely to be weak. While individual teachers may well be committed, there will be little social pressure encouraging student learning. Consistent with this argument, evidence shows that when teachers are able to interact, student learning increases (Ravitch 1995). In many American schools, however, teachers spend much of their day in the classroom with students—subject to the norms that students enforce. It is easy for teachers to become burned out when all they experience is resistant or, at best, passive students.

Research on the importance of peers (for both students and teachers) suggests that the problem with education does not lie completely with individuals and will not be fully remedied through penalties and incentives designed to motivate individuals. Rather, part of the problem may be that we have structured education so that teachers have little interaction with fellow teachers, they have relatively little power in the classroom (students are not dependent on them), and students spend the bulk of their time with others the same age.

Studies of education in other countries are consistent with this conclusion. Japan, for example, has often been praised for its educational accomplishments. Part of the reason for its success may have to do with the social structure of its education system.

Japanese students have historically been less dependent on each other and more dependent on their teachers than American students.[5] In general, youth culture in Japan is seen as weaker and less distinct from adult culture than in the United States. In schools, students typically stay in the same classroom throughout the day. At the elementary level, students eat lunch in the classroom with their teacher (Beauchamp 1989). Thus students interact more with their teachers and have to worry much less about navigating the social world of the school as a whole. In addition, students need their teachers—both in order to get recommendations for desirable jobs (Rosenbaum and Kariya 1989) and for gaining the knowledge that will help them do well on college entrance exams.

In further contrast to the United States, teachers interact with each other. They are assigned to desks in a single room (Rohlen 1983). They use the same materials and discuss teaching issues. They are therefore likely to be subject to greater levels of informal control from each other than are teachers in the United States. Further, ongoing relations between schools and employers provide additional motivation for teachers to produce good students (Rosenbaum and Kariya 1991). Competition with other schools to get students into elite universities increases pressures within the school to do a good job. Thus, in many ways the Japanese education system weakens relations between youths, encourages dependence of youths on teachers, and strengthens the social pressures on teachers to produce successful students.

Research on education in the United States and other countries such as Japan provides good reason to believe that social relationships matter for the enforcement of pro-education norms, and in turn, for learning. But in the United States, proposed government and market-based strategies say little about social relationships or the effects of policy changes on those relationships.

It is possible that standardized tests could increase student dependence on teachers. Students might pay more attention to teacher opinion if they needed the aid and expertise of teachers to help them pass those tests.

It is possible that market opportunities could increase dependence. Because students could choose, they would presumably end up studying with teachers they value.[6] It is also possible, however, that increased choice would decrease student dependence on their teachers—because students could always move on to another one.

We do not know. We pay relatively little attention to ways in which reforms affect the value of what teachers have to offer students or the social supports that energize good teaching. We seem to forget the very real constraints imposed by student norms (as opposed to a single student's or teacher's lack of ability or motivation).

If we believed that relationships mattered, then we would think explicitly about the structure of social relations in our schools. In addition to considering the most effective means of providing incentives to motivate individuals, we would think about how to strengthen relationships between students and adults. We would think about how to increase teacher interaction with fellow teachers so that they experience pressures from peers, not just from recalcitrant students. We would think about how to help students recognize the value of what teachers have to offer. Such an approach would avoid some of the weaknesses of government and market solutions. For example, it would not create incentives for teachers to cheat. And it might well contribute to the desired outcome—improved student learning.

In 2005, U.S. Senator Barack Obama told the story of a little girl, the child of a poor single mother, attending elementary school in Chicago (Obama 2005). She said, "I just study hard every night because I like learning. *My teacher wants me to be a good student and so does my mother. I don't want to let them down*" (emphasis added). As this little girl gets older, whom will she not want to let down? Her peers? Her posse? Her boyfriend? She is more likely to achieve if the people she does not want to let down understand and value education. How do government-mandated standards and market choices affect her relationships? How do they affect whom she does not want to let down? The most well-intentioned reforms may simply leave this girl at the mercy of her social environment.

Discussion

The discussion in this chapter suggests that the Amish may be on to something. Connections to governments and markets may indeed create the risk of weakening the social ties necessary for the maintenance of norms.[7] Groups that wish to remain cohesive may be wise to be wary of too much government largesse. And they should think carefully about the possible effects of market integration and the lure of efficiency on social relations.

I have argued that when governments and markets provide alternative sources of valued goods, they may weaken communities. I do not mean to suggest that we should therefore abandon them.

Governments do reduce violence (Cooney 1997). If groups are not working well, then withdrawing legal support risks creating a social control vacuum (consider post-Soviet Russia, post-Tito Yugoslavia, or post-Saddam Hussein Iraq). Further, centralized controls may be the most appropriate means of addressing certain kinds of problems.

Markets do increase wealth. Depending on the needs of the group, increasing wealth may be a high priority.

The point of this chapter is that reliance on governments and markets may have unintended effects. When evaluating a policy, it would be prudent to consider both the immediate effects and the ways in which that policy might impact social relationships. Policies may be most effective when they complement rather than weaken normative solutions. As we debate the relative merits of government command and control or market incentives, their effects on social relationships and norms ought to be part of the discussion.

8   Conclusion

DESPITE NUMEROUS EFFORTS TO DISCOURAGE FOOTBIND-
ing, the practice persisted for centuries. Chinese parents
apparently did not care much about legal sanctions or Western opinion.
Rather, they were concerned about their children's marriage opportunities. Footbinding disappeared only when parents were no longer afraid
that feet were relevant for marriage prospects—when Anti-Footbinding
Societies gave them confidence that their non-footbound daughters
would be able to get married and that their sons could freely marry
natural-footed women. The creation of Anti-Footbinding Societies was
a structural change that dramatically reduced the threat of social sanctions. Once these societies were in place, people no longer had reason to
comply with or enforce the footbinding norm.[1] Footbinding provides a
vivid illustration of the power of social pressure—of how concerns with
the reactions of others can lead people both to engage in harmful behavior and to compel others to do so.

The relational theory of norm enforcement similarly highlights these
concerns. People care about their relationships. They care about how
others think of them and treat them. They care about whether others
will marry them, or play hoops with them, or take them to the doctor, or

babysit their children. No one makes it alone. Because no one is an island, people have to consider the potential reactions of others.

The fact that people care about their social relations means that the characteristics and structure of those relations matter. How dependent are people? On whom are they dependent? These factors affect incentives to comply with and enforce norms. They lead people to sanction. And they affect metanorms. Metanorms—reactions to sanctions and expectations of reactions—affect norm enforcement. When social relations and metanorms vary, norm enforcement varies as well. As dominant theories suggest, the characteristics of behavior—its consequences, meaning, and frequency—affect norms. But they do so in conjunction with social relations and expectations of social reactions.

What Do We Learn from the Relational Theory of Norm Enforcement?

At the beginning of the book, I raised a number of questions:

- If a behavior is wrong or harmful, why is it sometimes punished and sometimes not?
- Why do people enforce norms that benefit others rather than themselves?
- Why do we see groups enforce norms far more than makes sense—so much so that they actually harm the group?
- Why do people punish nonconsequential behavior—behavior that has only trivial, if any, effects?
- Why do people sometimes sanction atypical behavior and at other times do nothing?

These questions are puzzling if we think that actors consider only a particular characteristic of behavior. They make sense once we recognize that people care not only about the consequences or meaning or typicality of a behavior, but also about how they are affected by others' interactions with them and, in particular, others' reactions to their sanctioning efforts. The fact that people care about their relationships means that norm enforcement does not just reflect the characteristics of behavior. It is also affected by the structure of social relations.

Harmful behaviors are unlikely to be punished if the social structures that support sanctioning are nonexistent. If social relations do support sanctioning, however, then we can expect enforcement to occur. People will enforce norms that benefit them. And, under appropriate social conditions, they will also enforce norms that benefit others rather than themselves.

Further, the fact that social relations matter means that norm enforcement efforts may not reflect behavior consequences and may be inconsistent with the costs and benefits of sanctioning. They can, for example, motivate people to sanction far more than is good for the group—reducing rather than enhancing group welfare. They can also lead people to punish nonconsequential behaviors—actions that have little if any effect. This will occur when something about the behavior (for example, the frequency with which it occurs and the meaning attached to it) provide clues that it is perceived negatively.

Of course, people may be wrong in their expectations of how others will react to sanctioning efforts. Consequences, typicality, and meaning provide information about potential reactions. But individuals may misread the clues. If they go ahead and sanction, *and they are in interdependent relationships*, they are likely to receive support for their actions. If so, then their misperceptions become a self-fulfilling prophecy. Misperceptions can lead people to enforce norms that nobody wants. (And enforcement patterns may change quickly if the social cues change.)

Metanorms and interdependence explain why sanctioning varies across different social situations. They explain why harmful behavior is sometimes punished and sometimes not. (Sanctioning varies not just with the consequences of behavior but also with social relations.) They explain why people enforce norms that benefit others rather than themselves. (Benefits are magnified through social relations. Further, individuals want to look like good actors, and one way to do this is to show that they care about others.) They explain why people enforce too much.

(The social rewards help to offset costs.) They explain why people punish nonconsequential behavior. (People use a variety of clues, not just the harm caused by a behavior, to figure out how others are likely to react to their sanctioning efforts.) And they explain why people sometimes punish atypical behavior and sometimes do not. (The meaning attached to the behavior matters and sanctions directed against it must be visible to others so that metanorms can operate.) A complete explanation of norms will consider not only characteristics of the target behavior but also the social networks in which people live their lives. Incorporating social concerns into our theories can help us understand why norm enforcement can seem so varied and so idiosyncratic.

Implications for Compliance

The theory outlined in this book focuses on explaining norm enforcement. Enforcement is an essential component of norms and is important for understanding compliance. This is because, if sanctioning never occurs, norms will fade—there will be nothing with which to comply.[2] But if norms are enforced, then people will expect violations to be punished. Both punishment and expectations of punishment can motivate compliance.

Just as norm enforcers consider the likely reactions of others, so too do norm compliers. To understand compliance, then, we need to explain both enforcement and people's expectations of enforcement. Those expectations will vary both with the characteristics of behavior and with social relations. Thus many of the arguments made in this book about why people enforce norms may also be useful for explaining why they obey them.

Consider gang membership, for example. Research shows that people in both high- and low-crime neighborhoods see gangs as destructive (Meares and Kahan 1998). But in high-crime areas 66% of teens believe that their peers admire gang members. In low-crime areas only 19% hold that belief. In turn, teens in high-crime areas perceive greater social pressure to participate in gangs. In other words, patterns of meaningful behavior affect expectations of social reactions, which in turn affect behavior. Social reactions and expectations of such reactions likely affect both behavior and sanctioning.

What Does the Relational Theory Leave Out?

Norms are a complex social phenomena. I have focused primarily on one characteristic of social relations (interdependence), and two mechanisms linking interdependence to norm enforcement (indirect benefits and metanorms). The theory and experiments described here explore just a piece of the complex norms puzzle. There is much that this theory does not address.

It does not explain, for example, why we feel so strongly about some norms—why we feel emotions like anger and disgust when they are violated. It does not explain the internal characteristics or feelings of individuals (such as guilt) that might motivate them to obey or rebel. The theory does not explain our conviction that we and others *ought* to behave in certain ways.

As philosophers point out, logic does not lead us from what is (the characteristics of behavior and social relations) to what ought to be (an internal sense of the rightness and wrongness of things). But human beings somehow make that leap nonetheless.

Research in evolutionary psychology provides one source of insight into why.[3] Evolutionary psychologists argue that, like other species, human beings are a product of evolution. Further, the brain, just like other parts of the body, was subject to evolutionary pressures. If this is true, then characteristics of human psychology have their roots in our evolutionary past—a past in which it would have been advantageous to us to have instinctive, emotional reactions to our surroundings.

Consider the human taste for sweets and fats. In the evolutionary environment, those who liked sweets and fats would have had a higher likelihood of surviving and reproducing than those who did not. They also would have had an advantage over people who tried to decide what to eat based on the evidence or on trial and error. People with a taste for sweets and fats were, therefore, more likely to pass on their genes to future generations. Those who did not like them probably had few descendants. As a result, human beings today have a taste for sweets and fats (a taste that is not necessarily advantageous in a modern world full of food).

Just as human beings evolved to have a taste for sweets and fats, we also evolved to have feelings about and preferences regarding others' behaviors. In particular, there is reason to think that human beings developed negative emotional reactions to behaviors that caused various types of harm.

In one memorable study, researchers trained monkeys to trade pebbles for cucumbers. Then one day they gave some monkeys cucumbers in exchange for their pebbles but gave others grapes. The monkeys who received only cucumbers became very angry at this unfairness (Brosnan and de Waal 2003). Among human beings, even small children can be heard to complain "but it's not fair."

Studies show negative reactions to other kinds of harmful behavior. Free-riding is a form of unfairness—people take benefits while relying on others to produce those benefits. And research shows that people get angry when others free-ride (Fehr and Gächter 2002). Further, they feel good when they punish such bad behaviors (Knutson 2004).

A perusal of research in evolutionary psychology, neuroscience, and other disciplines provides evidence that people are hard-wired to have negative feelings about harmful behavior. In essence, evolutionary psychology applies the consequentialist approach to our distant past.[4] Evolutionary pressures produced a brain that has emotional reactions to behavior consequences. In other words, evolution transformed an *is* (the consequences of behavior) into an *ought*. Neither the relational theory of norms (that relies on the characteristics of social relations) nor approaches that rely on the characteristics of behavior fully explain the *ought* component of norms. Evolutionary approaches contribute to our understanding by explaining the existence of a human brain with the capacity for moral outrage.[5]

Toward a More Complete Explanation

Research relevant for understanding norms does not always cumulate. In part this is because different approaches address separate pieces of the norms puzzle. Research on the characteristics of behavior tells us *what* is likely to be sanctioned; work on characteristics of the human brain helps us understand why human beings *feel* the way they do about it; and the relational theory of norm enforcement helps us understand the conditions under which individuals will *act* to respond to behaviors. If we explain how evolution has contributed to the hardwiring of morals, or if we explain how meaning is constructed, or if we identify the harm caused by a particular deviant behavior, we have not explained norms. Each of these efforts is just a part of the larger complex picture.[6]

Research should continue in each domain—the characteristics of behaviors, the human mind, and social relations. Further, work in each area should seek to identify the implications of its findings for norms, given insights produced by others. Behavior, the mind, and social relations are each only a piece of the puzzle. A complete explanation likely requires understanding of all three.

Conclusion

I have highlighted ways in which social relations and metanorms affect norm enforcement. Social relations are essential for understanding norms, yet are often neglected. As sociologists note, because people (including researchers) are individuals, it is easy for us to articulate the individual reasons for things. We are much less good at identifying social influences on our own behavior—or at recognizing the role of social relations more broadly. The theory and empirical evidence presented in this book show that social relations and metanorms do indeed matter for norm enforcement. Our understanding of norms will improve if we acknowledge their role.

The fact that social relations and metanorms matter has implications not just for research but also for policy. Debates often focus on the relative merits of market and government solutions—both of which treat people as atomized individuals. So too do efforts that focus on individual character and values. The relational theory of norms, by contrast, highlights ways in which social relations matter. Because relationships have a strong influence, government penalties, market incentives, and educational efforts directed at individuals may not have the desired effects.

Consider the case of footbinding. An obvious approach to changing the practice was to create legal penalties. In theory, such an approach would increase the costs of footbinding. Individuals would recognize those increased costs and change their behavior accordingly. But they did not.

Another approach was to change how people thought about footbinding, to educate them as to the consequences, and to let them know what the rest of the world thought of the practice. Individuals who recognized how awful footbinding was would surely change their behavior. But they did not.

Interventions directed at individuals did not work. The example of footbinding shows us that a focus on individuals may not be enough to produce change in the absence of social relations that support that change.

If we think that norms are deeply embedded in the human psyche or the local culture, we may despair of ever having much of an impact. If we think that norms are all about the characteristics of the behavior itself, we may use lots of resources in trying to educate people about those characteristics. But, if we recognize that norms are a product of social relations and expectations that can be changed, then we have another tool in our box of policy strategies.

In the 1900s, footbinding disappeared, almost overnight. When reformers created Anti-Footbinding Societies, expectations regarding social support for footbinding changed. Norms then changed as well, producing one of the greatest social transformations of the twentieth century (Mackie 2006). The discovery of how a Chinese community solved the problem of footbinding was, in many ways, a happy accident. Of course, such fortunate findings are always welcome. But, we may not want simply to wait for a lucky stumble. Perhaps, with more complete understanding, we can create the solutions we seek.

Appendix 1
Definitions

Cohesion: The mean level of dependence in a group.

Conformity: Individual behavior that is the same as that of the majority.

Dependence: The value that an individual places on a relationship with another person and the goods that the individual receives through the relationship.

Interdependence: The mean level of dependence between two people.

Legal Sanction: A punishment imposed by the government.

Metanorm: A specific type of norm that regulates sanctioning.

Metanorm Enforcement: The difference between reactions to people who sanction and reactions to those who do not sanction. Throughout the book I talk about this difference in terms of rewarding sanctioners.

Metanorm Expectations: Expectations that people have regarding how others are likely to react to their sanctioning behavior.

Norm: A rule, about which there is some level of agreement, that is socially enforced.

Norm Enforcement: Social sanction; a sanction imposed by an individual.

Normative Sanction: Social sanction; a punishment imposed by an individual. The individual bears the full cost of imposing the punishment.[1]

Sanction: The difference between reactions to people who engage in one behavior rather than another. Sanctions generally refer to either punishments or rewards. Through most of the book I use the term *sanction* as a synonym for punishment and for norm enforcement.

Typicality of Behavior: The frequency of a behavior in a group.

Values: Evaluative statements that are enforced internally. They do not require external sanctions in order to be effective.

Appendix 2

Methods

THIS APPENDIX PROVIDES ADDITIONAL INFORMATION RE-
garding the experiments described in the book. I summa-
rize the general recruiting procedures for all of the studies. I then describe
the three experimental games. For each game I give a general overview,
a description of the experimental manipulations and the measures of
the dependent variables, and the experiment instructions.

Recruitment and Procedures

I recruited subjects for all experiments by going to large undergraduate
classes and asking students if they would like to make money by participating in a study on social interaction. One of my research assistants
or I gave students a brief, general description of what they would be doing and distributed recruitment forms asking for contact information
and the days and times when each student was likely to be available. At
the end of the class, we collected the forms from students as they were
leaving.

The night before an experiment was scheduled to be run, we called
students to ask if they could participate the next day.[1] If they said yes, we

told them a time and place to meet us. We met the participants one at a time and escorted them individually to the lab. Once at the lab, each student sat in a separate room.[2] They neither saw nor communicated with each other before the experiment began (or after it was over). Even if they knew somehow that a friend or acquaintance was participating at the same time, they had no way of knowing to what position in the experiment that person was assigned.

At the end of each experiment, we paid subjects cash based on the number of points they had accumulated. They earned between five and thirty dollars, depending on the particular game, the conditions to which they were randomly assigned, and the choices that they and others made. Thus, subjects' decisions had real consequences—the money they took home with them. I or my research assistant answered questions from participants and escorted them individually from the lab.[3]

The Norms Game

Chapter 2: Experiments 1 and 2

In the Norms Game subjects interacted with each other in groups of four for forty-eight rounds. They made decisions about donating to one or more group projects. When individuals donated, everyone in the group was better off. Group members therefore were affected by the donation decisions of others. They had opportunities to sanction individuals who did not donate.

The Norms Game Framework

Groups of four subjects were randomly assigned to an experimental condition. Upon arriving in the lab, participants read detailed instructions on their computer screens. The instructions told the subjects that they were participating in an experiment on social interaction with three other people. They would be interacting with each other over networked computers. Everyone was assigned a letter for identification purposes—W, X, Y, or Z.

The instructions then explained all of the choices the participants would be making throughout the experiment. After everyone had finished the instructions, they completed some practice rounds. Then the experiment began. Participants did not know how many rounds there would be. They were told that the experiment would take two hours. In actuality it took about an hour and a half. Subjects therefore could not anticipate the final round.

The experiment was designed so that each round provided opportunities for consequential behavior (failure to donate) and for people to react to that behavior (give fewer points to those who did not donate than to those who did). Each round had four steps. Figure A.1 summarizes these steps from the perspective of actor W.

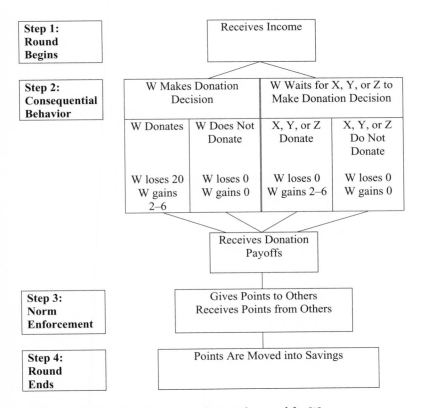

FIGURE A.1 Norms Game framework: Sample round for W

Step 1

The first thing that happened on each round was that every participant received 30 points. These points were placed in each individual's Personal Income box.

Step 2: Behavior with Consequences

Next, subjects either made a decision about allocating points to a group project or had to wait for someone else to decide. On each round, one person was randomly chosen by the computer to make this decision. A choice to donate to the project cost the individual 20 points. It also benefited fellow group members. If someone contributed to the project, everyone would receive a certain number of points—2 or 6, depending on the experimental condition. The points were placed in participants' Personal Income boxes.

Step 3: Norm Enforcement

After the allocation decision was made, each participant was able to give points to others and hope that others would give points to him. Subjects gave points to each other out of their Personal Incomes. They could keep any number of points they wanted as well as give any number of points to the three other participants. In making their decisions about giving points, subjects could take into consideration whether or not someone had donated to a group project. These exchange opportunities gave individuals the ability to express approval or disapproval of donation decisions—thereby enforcing norms about donations.

Subjects made their decisions about giving points simultaneously. Once all the participants made their decisions, they found out what others had given to them. Points they gave away were taken from their Personal Incomes. Points they received were added to their Personal Incomes.

Step 4

At the end of the round, all the points in each participant's Personal Income boxes were moved into his Total Savings. Once points were placed in savings, they could not be used. They accumulated throughout the experiment and determined subjects' earnings at its completion. After the point transfer, a new round began and subjects were again given an income of 30 points.

Experimental Manipulations

In the experiments that I conducted using the Norms Game, I manipulated interdependence and behavior consequences.

Interdependence (Experiments 1 and 2)

I manipulated interdependence by varying the value of points that subjects received from others relative to the value of their own. In the high interdependence condition, points received from others were worth two times the individual's own points. If X gave Y 10 points, Y would receive 20 points, and vice versa. If X and Y both gave each other 10 points, each would receive 20 points, for a profit of 10. In this condition, people valued their relations and the goods they could receive from those relations; interdependence was high.

In the low interdependence condition, points received from others were worth the same as one's own points. If X gave Y 10 points, Y would receive 10 points. If X and Y gave 10 points to each other, they would both break even. Here relationships had little value; social ties were weak. One might argue that this condition should be labeled "no interdependence" because subjects could do as well alone as they could by interacting. I chose not to use this label because subjects did have opportunities to exchange. Any individual's earnings therefore could be affected by others.

Behavior Consequences in Homogeneous Groups (Experiment 1)

In Experiment 1, subjects could contribute to one group project. I manipulated behavior consequences by varying the number of points that group members received if an individual donated to the project (and, correspondingly, how much they failed to gain if someone did not donate). In the small behavior consequences condition, every group member received 2 points. In the large behavior consequences condition each person received 6 points.

Behavior Consequences in Heterogeneous Groups (Experiment 2)

In Experiment 2, subjects were able to contribute to one of two group projects: G or P. I compared a situation in which everyone received the same benefits from donations to a project to a situation in which they got different benefits from contributions to two projects.

In the small behavior consequences condition, subjects chose whether or not to donate points to a single project. Every group member received 2 points if a contribution was made. In the large behavior consequences condition, subjects chose whether or not to allocate points to one of two projects. Majority members (X, Y, and Z) each received 6 points if a donation was made to Project G but only 2 points if a donation was made to Project P. The minority (W) received 2 points if someone contributed to Project G and 6 points if a donation was made to Project P. In other words, in the large behavior consequences condition, the majority wanted people to donate to G; the minority preferred donations to P.

Any individual who donated to either project lost 20 points. If no one donated to any project, group members neither lost nor gained points.

Measures of Norm Enforcement and Donations
In the Norms Game experiments, I measured donations to the project and norm enforcement (social sanctions). Below I describe the measures used in Experiments 1 and 2.

Donations in Homogeneous Groups (Experiment 1)
In Experiment 1, I measured donations by counting the number of times that group members gave to the group project over the course of the experiment. The more donations, the higher the group donation rate.

Norm Enforcement in Homogeneous Groups (Experiment 1)

I also created a group-level measure of norm enforcement. I did this by calculating the mean difference across all rounds between the number of points that subjects gave to individuals who donated to the project and to those who had the opportunity to do so but did not. The more points that people gave to the individual who donated as compared with those who had the opportunity but chose not to, the stronger the norm favoring donation.

The measure of sanctioning was based on the points that subjects gave, rather than on what the donator actually received. That is, I looked at the points that people gave before they were multiplied by one or by two. For example, assume that the mean sanction size (norm enforcement) in a group was 5. In the high interdependence condition, in order to determine the difference between what donators and non-donators actually received, one would need to multiply 5 times 2 (the exchange ratio) times 3 (the number of group members who could give points). On average, then, an individual who donated would receive 30 more points in a round than if they had the opportunity but chose not to. In the low interdependence condition, one would multiple 5 times 1 times 3. Donators would receive only 15 more points than non-donators.

Donations in Heterogeneous Groups (Experiment 2)

In Experiment 2, I measured majority donation by counting the number of times that X, Y, and Z donated to Project G. The more frequently they gave to the project, the higher the majority contribution rate.

I measured minority donation by counting the number of times that W chose to allocate points to Project G. The more frequently W gave to the project, the higher the minority contribution rate.

Norm Enforcement in Heterogeneous Groups (Experiment 2)

Majority norm enforcement refers to X, Y, and Z enforcement of a pro-Project G norm. I measured it by calculating the difference between the mean number of points that majority individuals gave to any group member who donated to Project G and to those who had the opportunity to donate but did not. The larger the gap between the points given to those who did and did not donate, the stronger the norm favoring allocation to Project G. I calculated a mean measure of majority enforcement for each experimental group.

Minority norm enforcement refers to the extent to which W enforced a pro-Project G norm. I measured it by calculating the difference between the number of points that W gave to people when they donated to Project G and when they did not.

When looking at the effect of pro-Project G norm enforcement on compliance, I used a measure of the group norm—norm enforcement by all four group members. I calculated the difference in points given by any of the four group members (W, X, Y, or Z) to those who contributed to Project G and to those who had the opportunity but did not contribute.

Norms Game Instructions

The instructions for Experiment 1 are presented from the perspective of actor W in the high interdependence, large benefit condition. The instructions for Experiment 2 were the same as those presented here except for differences due to manipulation of the behavior consequences condition.

Screen 1

Welcome to the Social Interaction Study

You and the other participants have been randomly assigned to an experimental condition. The condition to which you have been assigned, as well as the choices that you and others make, will affect the amount of money that you earn.

We are going to describe the experiment and let you make some practice choices. This will take about half an hour. Be sure to read carefully. You must understand the instructions completely in order to make money.

Throughout the rest of these instructions, click the Next button to get to the next page.

Good luck!

Screen 2

First, we will give you a brief overview of what you will be doing in the experiment. Then we will describe it in more detail.

You are participating in the experiment with three other people. You have been assigned to position W. The others have been assigned to positions, X, Y, and Z.

Screen 3

Each participant has two kinds of point boxes—a Personal Income box and a Total Savings box. At the beginning of each round of the experiment, everyone will receive an income of 30 points in their Personal Income box.

Screen 4

The Total Savings window is displayed directly below the Personal Income window. All the points you have at the end of each round of the experiment go into your Total Savings. Once points are put in your Total Savings, you cannot use them. They stay in your Total Savings until the experiment is over. You want as many points as possible in your Total Savings. The number of points in your Total Savings at the end of the experiment will determine how much money you will make. You will get one dollar for every 175 points that you have.[4]

Screen 5

During the experiment, you will have two kinds of choices to make.

1) Allocation Choice: You will be able to make choices about allocating points.

2) Interaction Choice: You will be able to decide whether to give points to others.

Screen 6

Allocation Choice

On each round after everyone has received their income, you or another participant will be given a choice about allocating points. You may decide to allocate points to the project or to keep them in your personal income box.

Screen 7

Allocation Choice

It will cost you points to allocate to the project.
However, you may also receive some points if you do so.

Screen 8

Allocation Choice

It costs 20 points to make an allocation. If you or anybody else contributes to the project, you will receive 6 points.

It costs 0 points to make no allocation. If you or anybody else makes no allocation, you will receive 0 points.

Screen 9

Allocation Choice

The next screen will show you what this decision will look like. To make your choice, click on the option you want. When you are finished, click on the Next button to finalize your decision and move to the next screen.

Screen 10

Allocation Choice

- Allocate points to the project
  (Cost=20, Receive=6)

• Do not allocate points
   (Cost = 0, Receive = 0)

Screen 11

Allocation Choice

You allocated points to the project.[5]

As a result of your decision, you lost 20 points and gained 6 for a total of −14 points.

14 points have been taken from your Personal Income.

Screen 12

Allocation Choice

If someone else makes the allocation choice, you will be asked to wait until that person has decided what to do.

After the other person has made a decision, you will be told what that decision is. Please go on to the next screen to see what this will look like.

Screen 13

Allocation Choice

__ has the opportunity to make an allocation choice.
Please wait for __ to decide what to do.

Screen 14

Allocation Choice

__ contributed to the project.
As a result of __'s decision
6 points have been added to your Personal Income.[6]

Screen 15

Interaction Choice

In addition to allocation choices, you will also be able to make interaction choices. You will be able to decide if you want to give points to X, Y, and Z. And they will be able to decide if they want to give points to you.

Screen 16

Interaction Choice

1 point from you = 2 points for X   1 point from X = 2 points for you

1 point from you = 2 points for Y   1 point from Y = 2 points for you

1 point from you = 2 points for Z   1 point from Y = 2 points for you

Every point that X gives you is worth 2 points for you.

This means that if X gives you 10 points, you will receive 20 points. And if you give X 10 points, they will receive 20 points. So if you give 10 points to X and X gives 10 points to you, you will make a profit of 10 points. X will make a profit of 10 points.

Screen 17

Interaction Choice

1 point from you = 2 points for X   1 point from X = 2 points for you

1 point from you = 2 points for Y   1 point from Y = 2 points for you

1 point from you = 2 points for Z   1 point from Z = 2 points for you

Every point that Y gives you is worth 2 points for you.

This means that if Y gives you 10 points, you will receive 20 points. And if you give Y 10 points, they will receive 20 points. So if you give 10 points to Y and Y gives 10 points to you, you will make a profit of 10 points. Y will make a profit of 10 points.

Screen 18

Interaction Choice

1 point from you = 2 points for X   1 point from X = 2 points for you
1 point from you = 2 points for Y   1 point from Y = 2 points for you
1 point from you = 2 points for Z   1 point from Z = 2 points for you

Every point that Z gives you is worth 2 points for you.

This means that if Z gives you 10 points, you will receive 20 points. And if you give Z 10 points, they will receive 20 points. So if you give 10 points to Z and Z gives 10 points to you, you will make a profit of 10 points. Z will make a profit of 10 points.

Screen 19

Interaction Choice

You may decide to keep all your points. You may decide to give all your points away. Or you may decide to give some away and to keep some. You may give more points to some people than others. You may give some people 0 points. The only rule is that you cannot give away more points than you have in your Personal Income.

Screen 20

Interaction Choice

When you make your choices, the points that you give away will be taken from your Personal Income.

After others make their choices, you will be told how many points you received from them. The points you receive will be added to your Personal Income.

Screen 21

Interaction Choice

The next screen will show you what this decision will look like. To make your decision, click on the box for the person you wish to give points to. Type in the number of points that you want to give. When you have done this for each person, click Next to finalize your decision and move to the next screen.

Screen 22

Interaction Choice

1 point from you = 2 points for X	1 point from X = 2 points for you
1 point from you = 2 points for Y	1 point from Y = 2 points for you
1 point from you = 2 points for Z	1 point from Z = 2 points for you

Keep ☐ points in your Personal Income

Give ☐ points to X

Give ☐ points to Y

Give ☐ points to Z

Screen 23

Interaction Choice

1 point from you = 2 points for X	1 point from X = 2 points for you
1 point from you = 2 points for Y	1 point from Y = 2 points for you
1 point from you = 2 points for Z	1 point from Z = 2 points for you

You gave __ points to X   You received __ points from X

You gave __ points to Y   You received __ points from Y

You gave __ points to Z   You received __ points from Z

Your total gain/loss is __ points.

__ points have been added to/taken from your Personal Income.

Screen 24

As the previous screen shows, after everyone has made their choices, the points you decided to give away will be taken from your income, and the points that others gave you will be added to your income.

Screen 25

After the interaction choice is made, the round is over.

All the points in your Personal Income will be moved into your Total Savings.

Then a new round begins. Each participant is again given a Personal Income of 30 points.

Screen 26

So, in summary, how do you make money?

You make money by making two kinds of decisions.

1) Allocation Choice: Decide whether to allocate points to the project.
2) Interaction Choice: Decide whether to give points to others.

The more points you receive as a result of your allocation choices and the allocation choices of others, the more money you will make. The more points that others give you, the more money you will make. Therefore, your earnings depend on your allocation and interaction choices and on the choices of other participants.

Screen 27

This is the end of the instructions. Before actually starting the experiment, there will be some practice rounds. You will practice making choices. Because this is just practice, the choices that others make won't give you any information about the choices they will make during the experiment. You will not be paid for the practice rounds and your decisions will not count. When everyone is done reading the instructions, the practice rounds will start.

If you are ready to start the practice rounds, click the Next button.

The Metanorms Game

Chapters 3, 4, and 7: Experiments 3–6, 9

In the Metanorms Game subjects interacted with each other in groups. They made decisions about punishing theft and about responding to the punishment decisions of others.

The Metanorms Game Framework

Groups were randomly assigned to an experimental condition. Subjects were instructed that they were participating in the experiment with four other people. Each actor was assigned a letter of the alphabet for identification purposes—V, W, X, Y, or Z. Participants were told that W, X, Y, and Z were all given the same instructions, but that V was given a different set of instructions and that they would not be able to interact with V. In actuality, V was a computer-simulated actor who stole points from other subjects.[7]

After everyone had finished the instructions, they all participated in some practice rounds. Then the experiment began. It consisted of fifty rounds.[8] As in the Norms Game, subjects were not told the number of rounds beforehand.

The experiment created harmful behavior. It provided subjects with opportunities to sanction that behavior and to react to others' sanctioning choices. Each round included five steps. Figure A.2 summarizes these steps from the perspective of actor W.

Step 1

First, as in the Norms Game, subjects saw a screen with a Personal Income box and a Total Savings box. At the beginning of each round,

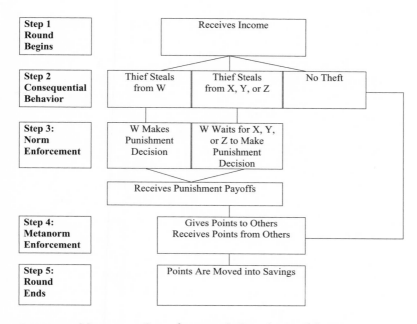

FIGURE A.2 Metanorms Game framework: Sample round for W

the computer automatically placed 30 points into each participant's Personal Income box.[9] Each person was given the same number of points.

Step 2: Consequential Behavior

Then, consequential behavior was provided by a computer-simulated thief. The participants saw a message on their screens telling them that V was making a decision and that they should wait while V decided what to do. On each trial V might steal from any one subject or no subject. The decision was generated randomly by the computer. On each round there was a 7/8 chance that the thief would steal. If V decided to steal from one of the participants, then that person lost 10 points. Those points were subtracted from the victim's Personal Income.

Every subject was a potential victim. Each person (even if not a victim on a particular round) knew that he could potentially be hurt by theft in other rounds and, therefore, had reason to disapprove of it.

Whereas the Norms Game created a situation in which the deviant was a member of the group, in the Metanorms Game, the thief was not a group member with whom participants could exchange. They could punish the thief but otherwise had no interaction with it. I structured the Metanorms Game this way in order to focus on the theoretically relevant causal connections. The metanorms argument highlights relations between sanctioners and other group members—not relations with the deviant. By eliminating exchanges between the deviant and others, I avoided extraneous variation that might muddy the results. Research shows that people are more likely to punish outsiders than insiders. We, therefore, might expect to see higher levels of sanctioning overall in the Metanorms Game than we would if the thief was a group member. But the theoretical causal factor of interest—interdependence—ought to have the same effect in both settings.

Step 3: Norm Enforcement

After the theft, the victim decided how to respond. In recent years, scholars have studied situations in which third parties, not victims, make punishment decisions. The purpose of many of these studies is to understand human psychological characteristics that affect sanctioning. I am interested in the effects of social factors that ought to work the same way for both victims and third parties. While victims may sanction more than third parties overall (Fehr and Fischbacher 2004), the effects of the casual factors of interest on sanctioning should be similar for both.

In my studies, victims of theft could decide to do nothing. Or they could decide to punish V. These two options were listed on the computer screen. Subjects made their sanctioning decision by choosing one of the two options.

If subjects chose not to punish, they lost no points and received no benefits. If they chose to punish V, it cost them points.

Subjects were told that if they punished, V would lose points. Thus punishing imposed a cost on the thief.

In addition, all four participants (including the sanctioner) would have points added to their Personal Incomes. After the victim made his sanctioning decision, all participants were told what that decision was. If a sanction was imposed, then points were added to each subject's Personal Income box.

This operationalization is consistent with the conceptualization of sanctioning as a response to a harmful behavior that produces benefits for group members. Everyone benefited from an individual's sanctioning effort. If the victim decided to do nothing, no one received any points.

Note that the benefit of sanctioning was the addition of points to each subject's income. The frequency of theft did not decline. I had two reasons for operationalizing benefits in this way. First, as a practical matter, if theft declined in response to sanctioning, subjects might soon be left with no deviant behavior to which to react. By controlling the level of deviance, I ensured that subjects had opportunities to sanction. Second, controlling the rate of theft made it possible to focus on the causal relations of interest without the confounding effect of change in rates of deviance. In naturally occurring settings, sanctioning and deviance covary, making it difficult to determine causal order. Here I control rates of deviance in order to study metanorm and norm enforcement.

Step 4: Metanorm Enforcement

After the victim made his sanctioning decision, all subjects were able to exchange points. Everyone, including the victim, could give any number of points from their Personal Incomes to any person, including themselves. They could reward the individual who had made the sanctioning decision, they could keep points for themselves, and they could give points to non-victims. Participants made these decisions at the same time. They made choices about giving to a sanctioner in conjunction with decisions about giving to other participants and about keeping points. They could use their knowledge of the victim's sanctioning decision as well as their experience from earlier trials in making their choices. Thus the decision to give points to a sanctioner represented both a response to a sanctioning decision and a part of a mutually rewarding interaction that might continue across many rounds.

After all participants had made their rewarding decisions, each individual's screen showed them how many points they had given to other subjects, and how many points they had received from each. Points they had given away were subtracted from their Personal Income display, and points they had received from others were added to their Personal Incomes.

Step 5

At the end of the round, all the points in each participant's Personal Income were moved into their Total Savings. Then a new round began.

Manipulation of the Experimental Conditions

In the experiments conducted using the Metanorms Game, I manipulated interdependence, indirect benefits, sanctioning benefits, sanctioning costs, and strength of the legal system.

Interdependence (Experiments 3–6, 9)

I manipulated interdependence in the same way as in the Norms Game. The higher the value of points that participants received from others relative to the points that they kept for themselves, the higher the level of interdependence. In the high interdependence condition, points from others were worth three times the amount of the individual's own points. In other words, if subject W gave subject Z 10 points, Z actually would receive 30 points. This meant that participants could do better if they interacted. They were dependent on each other. By contrast, in the low interdependence condition, points received from others were worth the same amount as points the individual kept for himself. So if W gave Z 10 points, Z would only receive 10 points. This meant that there was little benefit to exchanging. Subjects could do just as well alone as if they exchanged.

Indirect Benefits (Experiment 3)

In Experiment 3, in addition to manipulating interdependence, I manipulated the presence or absence of an indirect sanctioning benefit. I did this by placing the points that subjects received as the result of a sanction either into each participant's Personal Income or into their Total Savings. Points placed in subjects' savings accumulated throughout the experiment and could not be used for any purpose. They were "locked up" in a savings account and could not be withdrawn; they provided only a direct benefit. Points placed into subjects' Personal Incomes could be used for exchange; they provided an indirect benefit. This manipulation is consistent with the theoretical conceptualization of an indirect benefit as something that enhances the ability of individuals to engage in exchange.

In Experiment 3, sanctioning costs and benefits were not manipulated. In all conditions, the benefit of sanctioning was 4 points and the cost was 15.

Sanctioning Benefits (Experiment 4)

In Experiment 4, in addition to interdependence, I manipulated sanctioning benefits. I did this by varying the number of points that subjects received when someone sanctioned the thief. In the small benefit condition they received 3 points; in the large benefit condition they received 9. These points were placed in each subject's Personal Income box. In all conditions, the cost of sanctioning was 20 points.

Sanctioning Costs (Experiments 5 and 6)

In Experiments 5 and 6, in addition to manipulating interdependence, I manipulated sanctioning cost. I did this by varying the number of points that the victim lost if he decided to punish the thief. In the low-cost conditions (in both Experiments 5 and 6), the victim lost 4 points if he chose to sanction. In the medium-cost condition (Experiment 5), sanctioning cost 10 points. In the high-cost condition (Experiment 6), sanctioning cost the victim 20 points. In all conditions, the benefit of sanctioning was 3 points. This meant that in the medium-cost condition, the benefit to the sanctioner (3 points) was smaller than the cost (10 points), but the benefit to the group as a whole (3 points x 4 people=12) was greater than the cost. Sanctioning increased group welfare. In the high-cost condition, the benefit to the sanctioner (3 points) was still smaller than the cost (20 points). But there, the aggregate benefit to the group (3 points x 4 people=12 points) was smaller than the 20-point cost. The group was better off if sanctioning did not occur.

Cost was a within-subjects variable. Participants in each group experienced two levels of cost. Half of the groups experienced the low cost for the first twenty-five rounds and then the medium or high cost; half experienced the reverse.

Strength of the Legal System (Experiment 9)

In the strong legal condition, taxes were initially 20 points. Here taxes paid all of the costs of sanctioning legally and there was no personal cost associated with doing so. It was more costly to sanction normatively (10 points) than legally (0 points). In the weak legal control condition, taxes were initially only 5 points. Because taxes paid less of the legal institution's expenses, subjects incurred a higher personal cost of 10 points if they chose to sanction legally in the weak legal control condition than they did in the strong legal control condition. Thus in the weak legal control condition, the personal costs of normative and legal sanctioning were the same (10 points). This operationalization is consistent with the theoretical conceptualization of the legal system as an agent whose expenses are paid, at least in part, through taxes.

As subjects chose the legal option, taxes that maintained the system increased. Any one subject's decision had no perceptible effect. But the cumulative impact of the subjects' decisions increased everyone's tax burden. Specifically, for every legal sanction imposed, taxes increased by .2

points (and the personal cost of legal sanctioning decreased). The computer calculated and imposed the new tax every ten rounds. While taxes increased by .2 for each sanction, increases were rounded to the nearest whole number before being imposed on subjects.

Measuring the Dependent Variables

In the experiments that I conducted using the Metanorms Game, I measured norm enforcement (sanctioning), metanorm enforcement (rewarding), legal sanctioning, rewards, and the value of relationships at the end of the experiment.

Norm Enforcement (Experiments 3–6)

I measured norm enforcement by counting the number of times that sanctions were imposed in the group and dividing that by the number of sanctioning opportunities (the number of times the thief stole). This gave me a sanctioning rate for each experimental group.

Metanorm Enforcement (Experiments 3–6)

I measured metanorm enforcement by determining the mean number of points given to victims on the trials in which they chose to sanction and the mean number of points given to them when they chose not to sanction. I calculated the difference between the mean rewards given to victims who sanctioned and those who did not.

When I describe the mean rewards given to a subject, I am referring to the reward amount before it is altered by the exchange ratio, not the amount the person actually receives. Thus, in the low interdependence condition, a mean reward of 5 indicates that the mean amount that subjects gave the sanctioner is 5 points. In order to determine the amount the subject actually received, one would have to multiply that number by 3 (the number of subjects potentially giving rewards) and multiply the product by 1 (the exchange ratio in the low interdependence condition). In the high interdependence condition, one would multiply the number by 3 (the number of subjects), and further, multiply that product by 3 (the exchange ratio in the high interdependence condition).

Legal Sanctioning (Experiment 9)

To measure the amount of legal sanctioning, I measured the number of times that people chose to turn to the agent and divided that by the number of times that the thief stole. This gave me the rate at which each group used the legal system.

Rewards (Experiment 9)

I measured rewards by calculating the number of points that group members gave to anyone who punished the thief, whether they did so normatively or legally. This produced a mean reward level for the group.

Value of Relationships (Experiment 9)

At the end of the experiment, I measured the value that participants placed on their relationships with other group members—in other words, their perceived level of interdependence. Subjects saw a message on their computer screens telling them that they had an opportunity to change exchange partners. For each of the three other group members, they were asked how much they would like to stay with that person and how much they would like a new person to exchange with instead. Subjects entered a number between 1 and 9 to indicate their choice, with 9 indicating that they strongly wanted to stay with their current partner and 1 indicating that they strongly wanted a new partner. Subjects were told that the computer would take their answers into account in assigning new exchange partners. They believed that their answers would affect with whom they exchanged for the rest of the experiment. The questionnaire thus provided a behavioral measure of the value that subjects placed on their relationships with others. I calculated the mean value of all relationships for all subjects.

Metanorms Game Instructions

The screens below are presented from the perspective of actor W in the high interdependence condition with large sanctioning costs and small benefits. These are the basic instructions for all the Metanorms

Game experiments. There were minor differences across the experiments depending on the experimental manipulations.

Screen 1

Welcome to the Social Interaction Study

You and the other participants have been randomly assigned to an experimental condition. The condition that you have been assigned to, as well as choices that you and others make, will affect the amount of money you will earn.

We are going to describe the experiment and let you make some practice choices. This will take about half an hour. Be sure to read CARE-FULLY. You must understand the instructions completely to make money.

Throughout the rest of these instructions, press the PgDn key to continue to the next page of instructions, or press the PgUp key to review the previous page. Good luck and try to earn as much money as you can.

Screen 2

First, we're going to give you a brief overview of what you will be doing in the experiment. Then we will describe it in more detail.

You are participating in the experiment with four other people. You have been assigned to position W. You will be able to exchange points with three other participants who have been assigned to positions X, Y, and Z. The choices that you all make about giving points to each other will affect the amount of money that each of you earns.

One of you has been assigned to position V. On the next screen we will describe V's position.

Screen 3

V makes money by stealing from others. If the thief steals from you, you will be able to make a decision about how to respond. The choices that you and others make about responding to the thief will affect how much money everyone makes.

Because V is the only participant who steals, V has a separate set of instructions. You and the other participants will not see the instructions that V is given. V will not see the instructions that you have been given.

Screen 4

Basically, you have two kinds of choices to make. You make choices about what to do if the thief steals from you. And you make choices about giving points to others. The choices that you and others make will affect the amount of money that each person earns. Now we will explain the experiment in more detail.

Screen 5

Each participant has two kinds of point windows—a Personal Income window and a Total Savings window. In each round of the experiment, everyone will receive an income of 30 points in their Personal Income windows. Your Personal Income window is displayed in the top right-hand corner of the screen.

Screen 6

Each participant also has a Total Savings window. The Total Savings window is displayed directly below the Personal Income window.

All the points you have at the end of each round of the experiment go into your Total Savings. You want as many points as possible to be put into your savings. Once points are put into your Total Savings, you cannot use them. They stay in your savings until the experiment is over. The number of points in your Total Savings at the end of the experiment will determine how much money you make. You will get one dollar for every 180 points you have.[10]

Screen 7

In each round, after everyone receives their income, the thief will make a decision about stealing points. The thief can steal 10 points from any participant's personal income. If the thief steals from you, you will be able to decide how to respond. If the thief steals from other people you will have to wait for them to respond.

Screen 8

If the thief steals from you, you can do one of two things.

1)   You can punish the thief.

2)   You can do nothing.

Following is a description of these two options. You must understand these options in order to make money.

Screen 9

Option 1: Punish the thief

If you choose this option, points will be taken away from the thief. It will cost you 20 points to punish the thief. As a result of punishing the thief, you will receive 3 points. X, Y, and Z will each receive 3 points. The points you receive will be put in your Personal Income. The points others receive will also be put in their Personal Income.

Screen 10

Option 2: Not punish the thief

If you choose this option, nothing will happen to the thief.
It will cost you nothing and no one will receive any points.

Screen 11

When you are given an opportunity to punish the thief, you make your choice by using the arrow keys to highlight one of the two choices on the menu. After you have highlighted the option you want, press the Enter key to confirm your decision. On the next screen, make a choice about punishing the thief.

Screen 12

V stole points from you. Please make a decision to:

You punish V
>   It costs you 20 points
>   3 points are given to you, X, Y, and Z

No Punishment

>> Use the cursor arrow keys to select
>> You punish V
>> No punishment
>> Press Enter to confirm your decision.

Screen 13

You chose not to punish V.[11]

Your choice cost you 0 points.

As a result of your choice,
No points are given to you, X, Y, and Z.

Screen 14

If X, Y, or Z is given the choice to punish the thief, you will have to wait for that person to decide what to do. After the other person makes his decision, you will be told what that decision is. If the other person chose to punish the thief, you and the other two who were not stolen from will receive 3 points. The person who chooses to punish will receive 3 points. The points you receive will be put in your Personal Income. The points others receive also will be put in their Personal Income. The next two screens will show you what that would look like.

Screen 15

__ has an opportunity to punish the thief. Please wait for __ to decide what to do.

Screen 16

__ chose not to punish V.[12]
As a result of __'s decision,
No points are given to you, X, Y, or Z.

Screen 17

After punishment choices are made, everyone will be able to decide what to do with the points that are now in their Personal Income windows. You can do two things with these points. You can keep them or give them to others. V will wait while you decide what to do. Following is a description of these options. Again, you must understand these options in order to make money.

Screen 18

Giving points to others:

You will be able to decide if you want to give points to X, Y, and Z. In making this choice, you may consider whether you want X, Y, and Z to give points to you in the future. You may also consider their punishment choices.

Every 1 point that another person gives you is worth 3 points to you. This means that if another participant gives you 10 points, you will actually receive 30 points. And if you give another person 10 points, that person will actually receive 30 points. So if you give 10 points to another and he gives 10 points to you, you will actually receive 30 points. You will make a profit of 20 points (and so will the other person). The more points you get from others compared to what you give away, the more money you will make.

Screen 19

You may decide to keep all your points. You may decide to give all your points away. Or you may decide to give some away and to keep some. The only rule is that you cannot give away more points than you have in your Personal Income. When you make your choice, the points you give away will be taken from your Personal Income. After others make their choices, you will be told how many points you received from them.

Screen 20

The next screen will show you how to make choices about your points. You make a decision by typing the number of points you wish to give to another and then pressing the Enter key. After pressing Enter, you can use the arrow keys to move to your next choice. When you have finished making your decisions, press the F10 key to confirm your choices. To practice making this choice and to see an example of everyone's choices, please go on to the next screen.

Screen 21

1 Point from Giver=3 Points for Receiver

Keep	☐	points in your Personal Income
Give	☐	points to X
Give	☐	points to Y
Give	☐	points to Z

Screen 22

1 Point from Giver=3 Points for Receiver

You Gave:	You Received:
__ to X	__ from X
__ to Y	__ from Y
__ to Z	__ from Z

Your total change in personal income is __ points.

Screen 23

After everyone has made their choices, the points you decided to give away will be taken from your income and the points that others gave you will be added to your income.

All the points in your income will be moved into your savings.

Then a new round begins. Each participant is again given a personal income of 30 points. The thief makes decisions about stealing. Participants again make decisions about punishing the thief and giving to others. You will make these decisions for a large number of rounds.

Screen 24

So, in summary, how do you make money?

It costs you money if you punish the thief.

You make money if others give points to you.

In order to make the most money that you can, you must make your choices carefully. You can think about how your choices might directly affect the number of points you make. And you can think about how your choices indirectly affect the number of points you make by affecting what X, Y, and Z decide to do.

Screen 25

This is the end of the instructions. Before actually starting the experiment, there will be some practice rounds. You will be able to practice making choices and responding to the thief if he steals from you. Because this is just practice, the choices that other participants make won't give you any information about the choices they will make during the experiment. You will not be paid for the practice rounds and your decisions will not count. When everyone is done reading these instructions, the practice rounds will start.

The Expectations Game

Chapter 5: Experiments 7 and 8

Unlike the Norms and Metanorms Games, the Expectations Game was not computerized. Upon arrival, participants were individually escorted to separate rooms in the lab. They were told that they were participating in the experiment with seven other people. Each person had been randomly assigned to a position in the group (a letter between I and P). In actuality, subjects were always assigned to Position O and each participant interacted with simulated actors, not with fellow students. Subjects read instructions. Then the experiment began.

Overview

The experiment involved three tasks:

Step 1: The Survey Task

The first task was to answer five multiple-choice questions. These were questions like one might find on an I.Q. or vocabulary test. Only the subject (and the experimenter) knew their answers to the questions— nobody saw anyone else's responses. Subjects received points for answering the survey questions.[13]

Step 2: The Choice Task

The second task was to choose between two options. Specifically, subjects were asked to choose one of two letters, X or W. My intent was to create a behavior with no (or as little as possible) preexisting social meaning. This is not to say that the choice had no meaning at all to individuals, but that meaning varied. For example, one person associated X with women because women have two X chromosomes. Another associated it with men because men have an X and a Y chromosome. Although no experiment participant raised the issue, a colleague associated W with President George W. Bush, who is often referred to as, simply, "W." These associations appeared idiosyncratic, however. Participants expressed no common perceptions of choices. There was no evidence of shared meaning.

One might ask what can be learned from such an artificial task. As discussed in Chapter 5, in naturally occurring settings the meaning of a behavior and its frequency are often conflated. The researcher, therefore, cannot tell whether outcomes are due simply to patterns of behavior or to patterns of *meaningful* behavior. In order to distinguish between the effects of these two possible causal factors, I need to disentangle them empirically. I do this by initially creating a behavior that has no existing shared social meaning.

Other researchers use a similar strategy, creating artificial distinctions in the lab that do not correspond to meaningful distinctions in real life. When Tajfel (1982; Tajfel, Billig, Bundy and Flament 1971; and Turner, Brown, and Tajfel 1979) sought to study prejudice and discrimination, he did not look at existing dividing lines across which discrimination occurred—categories with existing social meaning such as race or ethnicity or religion. Rather he looked at "minimal groups," groups he formed based on arbitrary criteria. In his most minimal groups, he assigned subjects to "group X" or "group W" based on the flip of a coin (Billig and Tajfel 1973). He could then see whether mere assignment to a group would lead people to treat in-group members more favorably than those in the out-group. Here, rather than have subjects engage in behavior with existing social meaning, I had them engage in a "minimal" behavior. They chose between X and W. In the world, it is very difficult, if not impossible, to disentangle patterns of behavior, the meaning of that behavior, and sanctions regulating it. Lab experiments provide the opportunity to do so.

In the other experimental games, I examined a particular kind of artificial behavior—donations to a group project. That behavior had consequences for group members. Here I am interested in inconsequential behaviors. Thus, unlike in the Norms and Metanorms Games, the X–W behavior had no effects on others. It caused no harm.

Note that while the choice between X and W had no (or as little as possible) social meaning, this does not mean that subjects' choices did not matter. To the contrary, just as in the Norms Game, participants' behavior choices were visible to others. They knew that others could react to their decisions. Those reactions would affect their points, and in turn, the amount of money they took home.

The actors made their X–W decisions one at a time, starting with person I and moving in alphabetical order through person P. (In actuality, the decisions of all actors except for the subject were entered by the experimenter.) The subject (person O) was the seventh person to make a decision. This meant that subjects saw the decisions made by all but one person before they made their own decisions. Following the subject, P made its X–W decision. P always chose the atypical behavior, thus deviating from the majority. The number of points that subjects received for the Choice Task varied across conditions.

Step 3: The Evaluate Task

The third task was to evaluate group members' behaviors in the experiment. This task allowed subjects to sanction—to react to others' X–W choices. Subjects did this by giving each other person in their group between 0 and 25 points. As in the Choice Task, group members made their decisions one at a time. But here, the subject was the first to make a decision. As in the Metanorms Game, subjects' sanctioning decisions were visible to others.

Once subjects made their Evaluate Choice, the experiment was over. Participants were paid based on the number of points they had accumulated in the three tasks. Their earnings varied depending on the experimental condition to which they were randomly assigned and the decisions that they made.

Manipulation of the X–W Condition

Subjects saw a form in which the decisions of six other group members had been filled out. In the X condition, I through N had circled X. In the W condition, I through N had circled W.

Enforcement of an Anti-X Norm

After the X–W decision, subjects could decide whether to give points to other actors. They could give between 0 and 25 points to each other person. Giving points away did not reduce the subject's own points. I determined the size of the anti-X norm by calculating the difference in the number of points that conformers gave to those who chose W and those who chose X.

Expectations Game Instructions

Page 1

Welcome to the Social Interaction Study

The amount of money you make in this study depends on the choices that you and other participants make.

The more points you get, the more money you will earn. For every 65 points you get, you will earn one dollar. You can make up to $15.00.[14]

You must read the instructions carefully in order to make money.

To begin the instructions, please go on to the next page.

Page 2

You are participating in the experiment with seven other people. Each of you has been randomly assigned to an identification letter. Your identification letter is O.

This study involves three tasks:

1) Survey Task
2) X–W Task
3) Evaluation Task

You will be given instructions. Be sure to read carefully. You must understand the instructions in order to make money.

At any time, if you have a question, please slide the red question card out the door and the experimenter will come help you.

To read about the first experiment task, please go on to the next page.

Page 3

1: Survey Task

In the first task, you and all the other participants will answer five questions. There is one right answer for each question. Each question will be worth 50 points for a total of 250 possible points.

You will not know your score. And no one else will know your score. You will only receive information about the average score for your group.

If the average score is 5, you and the other participants will each get 250 points.

If the average score is 4, you and the other participants will each get 200 points.

If the average score is 3, you and the other participants will each get 150 points.

If the average score is 2, you and the other participants will each get 100 points.

If the average score is 1, you and the other participants will each get 50 points.

If the average score is 0, you and the other participants will each get 0 points.

To read about the second task, please go on to the next page.

Page 4

2: X–W Task

In the second task, you and each of the participants will choose between two options—X and W. The experimenter will bring around the X–W form to each person. All the participants in the study will make their decision one after the other using the same form.

To make your decision, find your identifying letter. Then circle EI-THER X OR W next to your identifying letter. After you fill out the form, the experimenter will take it to the next person.

You will receive 200 points for completing this task.

To read about the third task, please go on to the next page.

Page 5

3: Evaluation Task

In the third task, you and the other participants can evaluate each other. You do this by giving points. The experimenter will bring around the Evaluation Form to each person. All the participants in the study will make their decisions one after another using the same form. After you fill out the form, the experimenter will take it to the next person.

You may give each person between 0 and 25 points.

If you give someone 25 points, that means you think they are making very good choices.

If you give someone 0 points, that means you think they are making very bad choices.

You may decide to give everyone 25 points. You may decide to give everyone 0 points. Or you may give any number in between. You may give some people more points than others. When you evaluate another person, you can consider any choice they have made. And when they evaluate you, they can consider any choice you have made.

After you make your evaluation choice, the experimenter will take the form to the next person.

Page 6

This is the end of the instructions.

Please slide the GREEN card out the door and the experimenter will give you the first task.

REFERENCE MATTER

Notes

Chapter 1

1. Individuals affect others, both when they fail to contribute to the group and when they take something from it. Though one behavior is a sin of omission and the other a sin of commission, both affect the well-being of group members. (For research on how the two are perceived, see van Dijk and Wilke 1995; Haidt and Baron 1996; and Sell and Son 1997.)

2. Such individuals are "strong reciprocators."

3. Just as people react negatively to a harmful action, when a behavior produces benefits for group members, people will view it positively.

4. For an alternative perspective that also suggests that norms might help to overcome social dilemmas, see Kerr (1995).

5. There are a number of approaches to thinking about social capital. Social capital scholars regularly debate the meaning of the term.

6. I do not claim that social relations are the only influence on norm enforcement. For example, desires to eliminate behaviors with bad consequences play a role as well. But social relations are an important and poorly understood cause.

7. It may also be that the factors and mechanisms identified in the lab operate as predicted in the field but are a small influence relative to other, sometimes conflicting factors.

8. Cross-cultural experiments looking at how people play various games (the ultimatum game, dictator game, and so forth) show that people play them differently (see, for example, Gintis et al. 2005). These studies were designed to

evaluate the extent to which people in different cultures behave like self-interested rational actors. They show that people in different cultures do not view the games in the same way. But these results do not give reason to think that the theoretical factors of interest in my studies would have different effects in these cultures. Without information about possible interaction effects, there is little reason to choose a subject pool from one or another of these cultural groups. Future research should, however, investigate the utility of the ideas developed here across a range of settings.

Chapter 2

This chapter draws from my research published in 2008, "Norm Enforcement in Heterogeneous Groups," *Rationality and Society* 20(2):147–72 (a Sage publication), and in 2004, "Collective Benefits, Exchange Interests, and Norm Enforcement," *Social Forces* 82(3):1037–62.

1. Just as damaging behavior creates regulatory interests, so too do beneficial actions. People who are positively affected by a behavior have an interest in encouraging it. Sanctioning can be positive (encouraging desirable behavior) or negative (discouraging harmful actions). Most scholars, however, seek to explain negative sanctioning. Consistent with this existing literature, I focus on punishment. Accordingly, throughout the book I use the terms *sanction* and *punish* interchangeably.

2. This definition is drawn from social psychological research on power and exchange. Emerson's (1962, 1972) original formulation saw dependence as a function of both value and the number of alternative sources of the valued good: "Each actor is dependent on the other to the extent that outcomes valued by the actor are contingent on exchange with the other. This contingency is primarily a function of two variables, value and alternatives. B's dependence on A increases with the value to B of the exchange resources that A controls and decreases with B's alternative sources of the same (or equivalent) resources" (Molm 1997, 29). In this book I focus on variation in the value of relationships rather than alternatives.

3. Cohesion is defined in a variety of ways in the social sciences. Here I adhere to Emerson's (1962, 1972) formulation—cohesion is the average level of dependence between group members.

4. The indirect benefits of norm enforcement may be subtle. Sanctioning harmful behavior increases individual welfare. It also creates predictability. People can have more certainty about collective expectations and about how others are likely to behave. Without some level of predictability in social life, it

can be very difficult to function. Sanctioning can contribute to predictability, thereby facilitating interaction.

5. Demsetz's (1967) famous discussion of the emergence of property rights among the Labrador Indians provides an example of one way in which changes in dependence relations might interact with the consequences of behavior. A norm of property rights in Labrador gave people control over the rate at which the beaver supply was depleted. The direct benefit was that they could make sure that they maintained a beaver supply sufficient for their own use. The indirect benefit was that the norm protected a supply of beavers that could be used in exchange. By protecting that supply, property rights increased the ability of families to trade. When Indians traded only with each other, this indirect benefit was very small. Because they all had access to the same resources, they could do just as well alone as they could by interacting. They were not very dependent on each other. But, when fur trade with Europe opened up, Europeans offered goods that Indians could not provide for themselves. The transatlantic beaver trade was profitable. Accordingly, the indirect benefits of having access to a reliable beaver supply expanded. When those indirect benefits grew (due to new, valuable relationships), norms protecting property rights emerged.

6. One might call this the *no interdependence condition,* because subjects could do as well alone as by interacting. But subjects had opportunities to interact and their outcomes could be affected by others. I therefore call it the *low interdependence condition.*

7. The interaction between interdependence and consequences did not have a statistically significant effect. I therefore report the results of an analysis that did not include that interaction.

8. This result was observed during the last rounds of the experiment, after participants had time to learn that failure to donate resulted in fewer points from others.

9. Majority individuals received 6 points if a donation was made to Project G and only 2 points if a donation was made to Project P.

10. Minorities received 2 points from donations to Project G and 6 points from donations to Project P.

11. This effect is captured by the interaction of interdependence and consequences. Because the minority has only majority members to interact with, and because interdependence and consequences increase interaction, the minority's interaction with the majority is highly correlated with both.

12. Norms enforced by one category of people against another are an instance of disjoint norms (Coleman 1990). Examples include attempts by men to control women and by the wealthy to control the poor.

13. Research suggesting that the proportion of prosocial and self-interested individuals in a group affects sanctioning provides an additional explanation (Fehr and Gintis 2007).

14. Research suggests that while many people are self-interested, a substantial number are "strong reciprocators"—that is, they cooperate so long as others do so, and they punish failures to cooperate (see, for example, Fehr and Gintis 2007).

Chapter 3

This chapter draws from my research published in 2004, "Collective Benefits, Exchange Interests, and Norm Enforcement," *Social Forces* 82(3):1037–62, and in 2001, "The Enforcement of Norms: Group Cohesion and Metanorms," *Social Psychology Quarterly* 64(3):253–66.

1. Of course, reactions from others also create costs and benefits. Consequentialist arguments, however, tend to focus on costs and benefits associated with the behavior—and the benefits that come from discouraging harmful activities. Such approaches often do not focus on the reactions of others. Here I am specifically interested in those reactions and so I distinguish them from standard costs and benefits.

2. The official name of the church is the Church of Jesus Christ of Latter-day Saints. The term *Mormon* is a nickname.

3. Pitcher, Kunz, and Peterson (1974) compare family size among Mormons in Salt Lake City with those in California.

4. The same logic applies to relations between potential sanctioners and deviants. The more dependent people are on a deviant, the less likely they are to want to punish him. But if potential sanctioners have relationships with other community members, their interests in those relationships can overcome their fears of antagonizing the deviant, leading them to punish.

5. It may also have implications for debates in the religious literature about the effects of monopoly on a religion's success. For some of this debate, see Finke and Stark 1988; Stark, Finke, and Iannaccone 1995; and Stark and McCann 1993.

6. In 1960, Alvin Gouldner published a piece on the norm of reciprocity. That norm makes two demands: "(1) people should help those who have helped them, and (2) people should not injure those who have helped them" (p. 171). Is the theory described here "just" reciprocity in action? At some level, the answer is yes. The theory depends on the insight that people give to others who give to them. But, in and of itself, the fact that people behave this way does not

explain the production of collective goods such as norms. Consider the common wisdom that says that markets (exchanges between actors) are not good at producing collective goods like clean air. People may have a natural propensity to truck and barter (Smith 1776). But this natural propensity to exchange does not mean that people manage to produce collective goods. In fact, the frequent failure of bilateral exchanges to contribute to the larger group welfare is often identified as one of the weaknesses of markets. In this book I focus on social interaction rather than economic exchange, but it is by no means obvious that social interactions produce collective goods any more than do economic transactions. The argument made in this chapter and in Chapter 2 explicates how relations between individuals can facilitate the production of a particular collective good—norm enforcement. It explicitly connects "reciprocity" to norms.

7. Note that in the absence of an indirect benefit, the sign for the interdependence coefficient was negative rather than positive, though its effect was not statistically significant.

8. When sanctioning did not increase participants' ability to exchange, interdependence actually reduced norm enforcement (Model 3 in Table 3.3).

9. Here, metanorms appear to partially mediate the effect of interdependence on sanctioning. In another study metanorms completely mediated the effect of interdependence; when I included metanorms in the analysis, they had an effect on sanctioning and interdependence did not (Horne 2001).

10. Because subjects engaged in both sanctioning and metanorm enforcement, neither of these variables was manipulated. It is possible, then, either that sanctioning frequency affected metanorms or that metanorms affected sanctioning. The second possibility is more likely. There is little reason to expect sanctioning frequency to motivate the size of metanorms. It makes more sense that increases in the size of metanorms strengthened the incentives to sanction and therefore produced more norm enforcement.

11. Presumably, people will weigh the incentives associated with reciprocal rewards along with their desire to look good to third parties.

Chapter 4

This chapter draws from my research published in 2007, "Explaining Norm Enforcement," *Rationality and Society* 19(2):139–70 (a Sage publication).

1. Campaign against Political Correctness (2007) at http://www.capc.co.uk.

2. We cannot tell from the stories whether such enforcement is widespread in Britain or simply the idiosyncratic actions of eccentric individuals.

3. See Coleman's (1990) related discussion of zeal (pp. 274–78).

4. We would not expect this to continue indefinitely, of course. If someone is always a drain and never has anything to offer, eventually interaction is likely to decline.

5. At the beginning of the chapter, I described vignettes from a British Web site on political correctness. That Web site provides many examples of people not being able to use the word *black* to describe objects. The words to the children's song "Baa, Baa, Black Sheep" must be changed to "Baa, Baa, Happy Sheep"; a blackboard must be called a chalkboard; black pants are dark pants; and so forth.

6. Part of this dynamic may involve pluralist ignorance—people do not know what others think, they make the wrong assumption about others' beliefs, and they end up thinking that everyone believes something that, in fact, nobody believes. (For more discussion of pluralistic ignorance, see Centola, Willer, and Macy 2005; Kitts 2003; and Kuran 1995.) It may not always be clear, for example, just what constitutes racism and sexism—consider the white college student who does not ask questions in class because he is afraid of being labeled a racist. The relational theory of norms does not address the cause of such ignorance. But one could imagine that dependence relations might affect the extent to which people make an effort to understand what others think and thus be related to levels of pluralistic ignorance (for a related discussion, see Gruenfeld, Keltner, and Anderson 2003).

7. The mean sanctioning rate in the high interdependence/small benefit condition was .736. In the high interdependence/large benefit condition, it was almost the same at .809 (see Table 4.2). In interdependent groups, even when the cost of sanctioning was 20 points and the aggregate benefit to the group was only 12 points, norms were frequently enforced.

8. Additional analyses not reported here show no effect of the two experiments being conducted in different semesters.

9. I conducted an additional analysis to check for a possible curvilinear relationship between cost and metanorms. There was no such relation.

10. In the norm enforcement analysis, I initially controlled for the sequence in which subjects experienced the two costs and for the interactions of sequence with cost and interdependence. Sequence and its interactions did not have statistically significant effects on norm enforcement and including them did not change the results of the analyses. I therefore report the results without controls for sequence.

11. The drafters of the Uniform Commercial Code, for example, explicitly designed it to allow judges to import custom (see Bernstein 1996 for a discussion). More recently, others have suggested that the costs of law enforcement

might be reduced by taking advantage of informal controls (Kahan 1996). Instead of (or in addition to) putting someone in jail, a judge may order placement of a sign on that person's house or publication of his name in the town newspaper. The idea is that informal shaming can supplement legal punishment. For work by legal scholars suggesting that groups produce welfare-enhancing norms, see Ellickson (1991). For a different point of view, see McAdams (1997) and Posner (1996b).

Chapter 5

This chapter draws on my research appearing in "Metanorm Expectations: Determining What to Sanction," *Advances in Group Processes: Altruism and Prosocial Behavior in Groups* (Bingly, UK: Emerald Group Publishing, 2009).

1. Vegetarians and animal rights activists might object even to my eating a chicken. But disapproval for eating a cat would be much more widespread.

2. Ironically, however, as Experiment 4 shows, the benefits associated with sanctioning harmful behavior may not actually increase support for the sanctioner.

3. In some cultures, there may be norms about dressing warmly. During February travel in Central Asia, I was routinely scolded for inappropriate footwear (shoes instead of boots) and had people intervene to adjust my child's clothing to make sure she was warm enough. I do not know whether these were sanctions directed at an outsider who must not understand how to dress for cold weather or if such sanctions were also directed against locals.

4. While the Norse in Norway ate fish, those in Greenland apparently had not done so for centuries (Diamond 2005, 229–30).

5. Clothing seems to have been as well. Greenland fashions mimicked those of Europe (Diamond 2005, 246).

6. One might ask what can be learned from such an artificial task. As discussed above, in naturally occurring settings the meaning of a behavior and its frequency are often conflated. The researcher therefore cannot tell whether outcomes are due simply to patterns of behavior or to patterns of meaningful behavior. To distinguish between the effects of these two possible causal factors, we need to disentangle them empirically. I do this by initially creating a behavior that has no existing shared social meaning. In previous chapters, I examined a particular kind of artificial behavior—donations to a group project and thefts. Those behaviors had consequences for group members. Here I am interested in nonconsequential behaviors. Thus, unlike in the Norms and Metanorms Games, the X–W behavior had no effect on others. It caused no harm.

7. In these analyses I report only the sanctioning decisions of those subjects who conformed with the majority. I ran twenty subjects in each condition for an *n* of 40. But because not all subjects conformed, I ended up with a smaller number in the analyses.

8. For discussion of pluralistic ignorance and social norms, see Centola, Willer, and Macy 2005; Kitts 2003; and Kuran 1995.

9. "[I]f voters have become more polarized over time we should see an increase in the number of voters predicted to vote for one candidate with very high probability and the other candidate with very low probability, or equivalently, a decrease in voters with probabilities of voting for the two candidates that are close to 50:50" (Fiorina, Abrams, and Pope 2006, 46–47). But this has not happened.

10. This distortion may be even larger when highly prominent individuals express extreme views—contributing to the perception that many people hold those views.

Chapter 6

The discussion of sex norms draws from my research published in 2004, "Values and Evolutionary Psychology," *Sociological Theory* 22(3):477–503.

1. The relational theory suggests that when people are dependent on a sanctioner, they will give support. It is also likely that the more dependent a sanctioner is on others, the more concerned he will be about their potential reactions.

Chapter 7

This chapter draws from my research published in 2001, "Community and the State: The Relationship between Normative and Legal Controls." *European Sociological Review* 16(3):225–43 (an Oxford Journals publication).

1. Amish communities vary in the details of their rules. For a more complete description of Amish life, see Hostetler 1993; and Kraybill 1989, 1993.

2. This view of the legal system as activated by individual complaints is consistent with empirical reality. While the state occasionally initiates its own independent investigations, legal processing of criminal and civil matters typically is instigated by individuals (Black 1973; Jhering 1879; Jones 1969; Pound 1917).

3. Edward Lawler and his colleagues make a similar argument. They suggest that certain interaction structures strengthen relationships, and, in particular,

that they build emotional cohesion (see Lawler, Thye, and Yoon 2008 for an overview of this research; see also Molm, Collett, and Schaefer 2007 and Molm, Schaefer, and Collett 2007 for related work). Here I suggest that interactions centered around sanctioning also strengthen relationships.

4. Absolute wealth may not be the driving factor. Rather, individuals' perceptions that they are doing well (based on comparisons with others or their own pasts), not their actual resources, drive their inclination to care about others.

5. For descriptions of the Japanese education system, see Lynn 1988; and Rohlen 1983.

6. Psychological research provides evidence that people express more satisfaction with outcomes when they had a choice than when they had no choice.

7. In the nineteenth and twentieth centuries, for example, workers were right to be wary of benefits provided by employers and by government. Those benefits weakened mutual aid societies that had been an important source of support for workers. Relationships deteriorated. As Beito (2000) writes, "The shift from mutual aid and self-help to the welfare state has involved more than a simple booking transfer of service provision from one set of institutions to another. As many of the leaders of fraternal societies had feared, much was lost in an exchange that transcended monetary calculations. The old relationships of voluntary reciprocity . . . have slowly given way . . ." (p. 234).

Chapter 8

1. It is conceivable that the government could have imposed a social sanction in this instance—for example, making it illegal for anyone to marry a footbound woman. But law is a blunt and limited tool for imposing social sanctions. There are many kinds of interpersonal sanctions that government is not in a position to enforce.

2. For a related discussion, see Kerr (1999).

3. For a discussion of basic evolutionary principles, see Miller and Kanazawa 2007.

4. Some evolutionary research suggests that morals do not just reflect concern with harm but with other issues such as purity and respect for authority. (See, for example, Haidt and Graham 2007; Haidt, Koller, and Dias 1993; and Rozin et al. 1999.) These morals may have been connected to harm in the evolutionary environment. People who did not have a concern for purity, for example, might have been more likely to get food poisoning or contract a contagious disease. In today's world, however, such concerns are often disconnected from the consequences of behavior.

5. Understanding of evolutionary pressures may also be useful for explaining the content of normative rules. Human beings may have a brain that is more attuned to some kinds of behaviors than others. For example, fear appears to be partly learned and partly biological. Researchers have shown that if they expose a baby monkey to an adult who is afraid of snakes, the baby learns to fear snakes. But if they expose a baby monkey to an adult who is afraid of flowers, the baby pays little attention (Öman and Mineka 2001). Other research shows that people are highly attuned to cheating. Human beings are not very good at solving logic problems. We make lots of mistakes. But when the logic problem involves cheating, responses are very consistent (Cosmides and Tooby 1992). Such work shows that the brain is primed to be attuned to particular kinds of behaviors. Thus it is likely that some combination of understanding of the human brain in conjunction with understanding of processes through which people construct meaning and evaluate the consequences of behaviors will lead to valuable insights regarding the content of normative rules.

6. This description of how different bodies of research connect is oversimplified, of course. For example, the consequences of behavior, not just social relations, can provide incentives to sanction. Work on characteristics of the human brain may tell us something about the types of behavior that are likely to become normative, as well as explain emotional reactions to them.

Appendix 1

1. Not all punishments imposed by individuals are instances of norm enforcement. Norms require some level of consensus. Therefore idiosyncratic punishments by lone individuals do not constitute norm enforcement.

Appendix 2

1. In all nine experiments there were equal numbers of male and female participants.

2. The one exception to this was Experiment 9. That study was conducted in a large room with many computers separated by partitions.

3. I provided additional written debriefing materials to participants in Experiment 8. These materials explained that there was no research finding that people's line preferences were correlated with the number of friends they had.

4. This was the point-to-dollar ratio in Experiment 1. In Experiment 2, subjects received a dollar for every 175 points.

5. Here I assume that W chose to allocate points. During the experiment, subjects chose to donate or not. Screen 11 reflected their choices.

6. This screen shows what W would see if another participant decided to allocate points. If another person chose not to allocate points, this screen would reflect that choice.

7. Subjects expressed no suspicion that actor V might not be a real person. In fact, to the extent that a few people expressed any suspicion, it was directed at the other three (student) actors. A few people thought that the other actors' decisions were so foolish that they could not have been made by real people.

8. Experiment 4 had 25 rounds.

9. In Experiment 9, subjects received 50 points of personal income.

10. This was the point-to-dollar ratio in Experiment 3. In Experiments 4, 5, and 6, subjects received one dollar for every 180 points they earned. In Experiment 9 they received one dollar for every 250 points.

11. This assumes that W chose not to punish. In the experiment subjects might choose to punish or not. Screen 13 reflected their choice.

12. This screen illustrates what W saw if another participant chose not to punish. If another person chose to punish, this screen would reflect that choice.

13. Both the survey task and the choice task were used to manipulate intergroup conflict.

14. In Experiments 7 and 8, subjects could make a maximum of $10.00. In other experiments run using these instructions, but manipulating other conditions, subjects could make the $15.00 described. The recruitment forms told potential participants that the amount they made would vary depending on the condition to which they were randomly assigned and the decisions that they and other participants made.

References

Abbott, Kenneth W., and Duncan Snidal. 2000. "Hard and Soft Law in International Governance." *International Organizations* 54(3):421–56.

Abrahamson, Eric, and Lori Rosenkopf. 1993. "Institutional and Competitive Bandwagons: Using Mathematical Modeling as a Tool to Explore Innovation Diffusion." *Academy of Management Review* 18(3):487–517.

Asch, Solomon E. 1951. "Effects of Group Pressure upon the Modification and Distortion of Judgments." Pp. 177–90 in *Groups, Leadership, and Men*, edited by H. Guetzkow. Pittsburgh, PA: Carnegie Mellon University Press.

Axelrod, Robert. 1986. "An Evolutionary Approach to Norms." *American Political Science Review* 80(4):1095–111.

Ballard, M. Russell. 2007. "Faith, Family, Facts, and Fruit." The Church of Jesus Christ of Latter-day Saints. http://www.lds.org/conference/talk/display/0, 5232,23-1-775-9,00.html (accessed July 18, 2008).

Banerjee, Abhijit V. 1992. "A Simple Model of Herd Behavior." *The Quarterly Journal of Economics* 107(3):797–817.

Beauchamp, Edward. 1989. "Education." Pp. 225–51 in *Democracy in Japan*, edited by T. Ishida and E. S. Krauss. Pittsburgh, PA: University of Pittsburgh Press.

Beito, David T. 2000. *From Mutual Aid to the Welfare State: Fraternal Societies and Social Services, 1890–1967.* Chapel Hill, NC: University of North Carolina Press.

Benard, Stephen . 2007a. "Group Conflict, Cultural Values, and the Emergence of Norms and Hierarchies." Unpublished manuscript.

———. 2007b. Personal communication, June 2007.

Berger, Peter L., and Thomas Luckmann. 1967. *The Social Construction of Reality*. New York: Doubleday Anchor.

Bernstein, Lisa. 1992. "Opting Out of the Legal System: Extralegal Contractual Relations in the Diamond Industry." *Journal of Legal Studies* 21(1):115–57.

———. 1996. "Merchant Law in a Merchant Court: Rethinking the Code's Search for Immanent Business Norms." *University of Pennsylvania Law Review* 144:1765–821.

Bicchieri, Cristina. 2006. *The Grammar of Society: The Nature and Dynamics of Social Norms*. Cambridge: Cambridge University Press.

Billig, Michael, and Henri Tajfel. 1973. "Social Categorization and Similarity in Intergroup Behavior." *European Journal of Social Psychology* 3(1):27–52.

Black, Donald. 1973. "The Mobilization of Law." *Journal of Legal Studies* 2:125–49.

Blood, Robert O., and Donald M. Wolfe. 1960. *Husbands and Wives: The Dynamics of Married Living*. New York: Free Press.

Bornstein, Gary, and Meyrev Ben-Yossef. 1994. "Cooperation in Intergroup and Single-group Social Dilemmas." *Journal of Experimental Social Psychology* 30:52–67.

Bourdieu, Pierre. 2000. "Making the Economic Habitus: Algerian Workers Revisited." *Ethnography* 1:17–41.

Brennan, Geoffrey, and Philip Pettit. 2004. *The Economy of Esteem: An Essay on Civil and Political Society*. Oxford: Oxford University Press.

Brewer, Marilyn. 1979. "In-group Bias in the Minimal Intergroup Situation: A Cognitive Motivational Analysis." *Psychological Bulletin* 86:307–24.

Brewer, Marilyn, and Roderick Kramer. 1985. "The Psychology of Intergroup Attitudes and Behavior." *Annual Review of Psychology* 36:219–43.

Brosnan, Sarah F., and Frans B. M. de Waal. 2003. "Monkeys Reject Unequal Pay." *Nature* 425:297–99.

Bryk, Anthony S., Valerie E. Lee, and Julia B. Smith. 1990. "High School Organization and Its Effects on Teachers and Students: An Interpretive Summary of the Research." Pp. 135–226 in *Choice and Control in American Education, Volume 1: The Theory of Choice and Control in Education*, edited by W. H. Clune and J. F. Witte. London: The Falmer Press.

Bursik, Robert J., Jr., and Harold G. Grasmick. 1993. *Neighborhoods and Crime*. New York: Lexington Books.

Campaign Against Political Correctness. http://www.capc.co.uk (accessed July 22, 2008).

Centola, Damon, Robb Willer, and Michael Macy. 2005. "The Emperor's Dilemma: A Computational Model of Self-Enforcing Norms." *American Journal of Sociology* 110:1009–40.

Chwe, Michael Suk-Young. 2001. *Rational Ritual: Culture, Coordination, and Common Knowledge.* Princeton, NJ: Princeton University Press.

Cialdini, Robert B. 2007. "Descriptive Social Norms as Underappreciated Sources of Social Control." *Psychometrika* 72(2):263–68.

Cialdini, Robert B., Carl A. Kallgren, and Raymond R. Reno. 1991. "A Focus Theory of Normative Conduct: A Theoretical Refinement and Reevaluation of the Role of Norms in Human Behavior." *Advances in Experimental Social Psychology* 21:201–34.

Cialdini, Robert B., and Melanie R. Trost. 1998. "Social Influence: Social Norms, Conformity, and Compliance." Pp. 151–92 in *The Handbook of Social Psychology,* edited by D. T. Gilbert, S. T. Fiske, and G. Lindzey. Boston, MA: McGraw-Hill.

Cohen, Dov, and Joe Vandello. 1998. "Meanings of Violence." *Journal of Legal Studies* 27(2):567–84.

Cohen, Jean L. 1985. "Strategy or Identity: New Theoretical Paradigms and Contemporary Social Movements." *Social Research* 52(4):663–716.

Cole, Wade. 2005. "Sovereignty Relinquished? Explaining Commitment to the International Human Rights Covenants, 1966–1999." *American Sociological Review* 70(3):472–95.

Coleman, James S. 1961. *The Adolescent Society.* New York: Free Press.

———. 1966. "Female Status and Premarital Sexual Codes." *American Journal of Sociology* 72:217.

———. 1990. *Foundations of Social Theory.* Cambridge, MA: Harvard University Press.

Cooney, Mark. 1997. "From Warre to Tyranny: Lethal Conflict and the State." *American Sociological Review* 62(2):316–38.

Corsaro, William A. 1985. *Friendship and Peer Culture in the Early Years.* Norwood, NJ: Ablex Publishing.

Cosmides, Leda, and John Tooby. 1992. "Cognitive Adaptations for Social Exchange." Pp. 163–228 in *The Adapted Mind: Evolutionary Psychology and the Generation of Culture.* New York: Oxford University Press.

Cosmides, Leda, John Tooby, and Robert Kurzban. 2003. "Perceptions of Race." *Trends in Cognitive Science* 7(4):173–79.

Croll, Elisabeth. 1990. *Wise Daughters of Foreign Lands: European Women Writers in China.* New York: Routledge.

Cusick, Philip A. 1973. *Inside High School: The Student's World.* New York: Holt, Rinehart and Winston.

Davies, Bronwyn. 1982. *Life in the Classroom and Playground: The Accounts of Primary School Children*. London: Routledge and Kegan Paul.

Demsetz, Harold. 1967. "Toward a Theory of Property Rights." *American Economic Review* 57:347–59.

Dennen, Johan M. G. van der, and Vincent Falger. 1990. *Sociobiology and Conflict: Evolutionary Perspectives on Competition, Cooperation, Violence, and Warfare*. London: Chapman and Hall.

Deutsch, Morton, and Harold B. Gerard. 1955. "A Study of Normative and Informational Social Influences upon Individual Judgment." *Journal of Abnormal and Social Psychology* 51: 629–36.

Diamond, Jared. 2005. *Collapse: How Societies Choose to Fail or Succeed*. New York: Penguin Books.

Diamond, Stanley. 1971. "The Rule of Law Versus the Order of Custom." *Social Research* 38:42–72.

DiMaggio, Paul, John Evans, and Bethany Bryson. 1996. "Have Americans' Social Attitudes Become More Polarized?" *American Journal of Sociology* 102(3):690–755.

DiMaggio, Paul J., and Walter W. Powell. 1983. "The Iron Cage Revisited: Institutional Isomorphism and Collective Rationality in Organizational Fields." *American Sociological Review* 48:147–60.

Dobbin, Frank. 1994. *Forging Industrial Policy: The United States, Britain, and France in the Railway Age*. Cambridge: Cambridge University Press.

Durkheim, Emile. 1951. *Suicide*. New York: Free Press.

Earls, Felton. 1999. *Project on Human Development in Chicago Neighborhoods: Community Survey, 1994–1995*. (Computer file). ICPSR version. Boston, MA: Harvard Medical School (producer), 1997. Ann Arbor, MI: Interuniversity Consortium for Political and Social Research (distributor), 1999.

Eckhardt, Kenneth W. 1971. "Exchange Theory and Sexual Permissiveness." *Behavior Science Notes* 6:1–18.

Elias, Norbert. 2000. *The Civilizing Process*. Oxford: Blackwell Publishing.

Ellickson, Robert C. 1991. *Order Without Law: How Neighbors Settle Disputes*. Cambridge, MA: Harvard University Press.

———. 2001. "The Evolution of Norms: A Perspective from the Legal Academy." Pp. 35–75 in *Social Norms*, edited by Michael Hechter and Karl-Dieter Opp. New York: Russell Sage.

Ellison, Christopher G., and Darren E. Sherkat. 1995. "The 'Semi-Involuntary Institution' Revisited: Regional Variations in Church Participation among Black Americans." *Social Forces* 73(4):1415–37.

———. 1999. "Identifying the Semi-Involuntary Institution: A Clarification." *Social Forces* 78(2):793–800.

Elster, Jon. 1989. *The Cement of Society: A Study of Social Order*. Cambridge: Cambridge University Press.

———. 1990. "Norms of Revenge." *Ethics* 100:862–85.

Emerson, Richard M. 1962. "Power-Dependence Relations." *American Sociological Review* 27(1):31–41.

———. 1972. "Exchange Theory, Part II: Exchange Relations and Networks." Pp. 58–87 in *Sociological Theories in Progress*, vol. 2, edited by J. Berger, M. Zelditch, Jr., and B. Anderson. Boston, MA: Houghton Mifflin.

Epstein, Joyce L. 1983. "The Influence of Friends on Achievement and Affective Outcomes." Pp. 177–200 in *Friends in School: Patterns of Selection and Influence in Secondary Schools*, edited by J. L. Epstein and N. Karweit. New York: Academic Press.

Everhart, Robert B. 1983. *Reading, Writing, and Resistance: Adolescence and Labor in a Junior High School*. Boston, MA: Routledge and Kegan Paul.

Eyre, Dana P., and Mark C. Suchman. 1996. "Status, Norms, and the Proliferation of Conventional Weapons: An Institutional Theory Approach." Pp. 79–113 in *The Culture of National Security*, edited by Peter J. Katzenstein. New York: Columbia University Press.

Fehr, Ernst, and Urs Fischbacher. 2004. "Third-Party Punishment and Social Norms." *Evolution and Human Behavior* 25:63–87.

Fehr, Ernst, and Simon Gächter. 2002. "Altruistic Punishment in Humans." *Nature* 415:137–40.

Fehr, Ernst, and Herbert Gintis. 2007. "Human Motivation and Social Cooperation: Experimental and Analytical Foundations." *Annual Review of Sociology* 33:43–64.

Felson, Richard B. 2000. "The Normative Protection of Women from Violence." *Sociological Forum* 15(1):91–116.

Ferrara, Peter J. 1993. "Social Security and Taxes." Pp. 125–43 in *The Amish and the State*, edited by D. B. Kraybill. Baltimore, MD: Johns Hopkins University Press.

Fine, Gary Alan. 1987. *With the Boys: Little League Baseball and Preadolescent Culture*. Chicago, IL: University of Chicago Press.

———. 2001. "Enacting Norms: Mushrooming and the Culture of Expectations and Explanations." Pp. 139–64 in *Social Norms*, edited by Michael Hechter and Karl-Dieter Opp. New York: Russell Sage.

Finke, Roger, and Rodney Stark. 1988. "Religious Economies and Sacred Canopies: Religious Mobilization in American Cities, 1906." *American Sociological Review* 53:41–49.

Finnemore, Martha. 1996a. "Norms, Culture, and World Politics: Insights from Sociology's New Institutionalism." *International Organization* 50(2):325–47.

——. 1996b. "Constructing Norms of Humanitarian Intervention." Pp. 151–85 in *The Culture of National Security*, edited by P. J. Katzenstein. New York: Columbia University Press.

Finnemore, Martha, and Kathryn Sikkink. 1998. "International Norm Dynamics and Political Change." *International Organization* 52(4):887–917.

Fiorina, Morris P., with Samuel J. Abrams, and Jeremy C. Pope. 2006. *Culture War? The Myth of a Polarized America*. New York: Pearson Longman.

Flache, Andreas. 1996. *The Double Edge of Networks*. Amsterdam, The Netherlands: Thesis Publishers.

Flache, Andreas, and Michael Macy. 1996. "The Weakness of Strong Ties: Collective Action Failure in a Highly Cohesive Group." *Journal of Mathematical Sociology* 21(1):3–28.

Fordham, Signithia, and John U. Ogbu. 1986. "Black Students' Success: Coping with the 'Burden of Acting White.'" *The Urban Review* 18:176–206.

Fourcade, Marion, and Kieran Healy. 2007. "Moral Views of Market Society." *Annual Review of Sociology* 33:285–311.

Frauenfelder, Mark. 2001. "The Year in Ideas: A to Z: Social-Norms Marketing." *The New York Times*, December 9, 2001.

Frey, Bruno S., and Alois Stutzer. 2002. *Happiness and Economics: How the Economy and Institutions Affect Human Well-being*. Princeton, NJ: Princeton University Press.

Friedman, Benjamin M. 2005. *The Moral Consequences of Economic Growth*. New York: Alfred A. Knopf.

Fussell, Elizabeth. 2008. "Social Networks in Disaster." Unpublished manuscript.

Futrell, Robert, and Pete Simi. 2004. "Free Spaces, Collective Identity, and the Persistence of U.S. White Power Activism." *Social Problems* 51(1):16–42.

Gale, Douglas. 1996. "What Have We Learned from Social Learning?" *European Economic Review* 40:617–28.

Gellner, Ernest. 1988. "Trust, Cohesion, and the Social Order." In *Trust: Making and Breaking Cooperative Relations*, edited by Diego Gambetta. New York: Basil Blackwell.

Gintis, Herbert, Samuel Bowles, Robert Boyd, and Ernst Fehr. 2005. *Moral Sentiments and Material Interests: The Foundations of Cooperation in Economic Life*. Cambridge, MA: The MIT Press.

Glenn, Brian J. 2001. "Collective Precommitment from Temptation: The Amish and Social Security." *Rationality and Society* 13(2):185–204.

Goffman, Erving. 1959. *Presentation of Self in Everyday Life*. Garden City, NY: Anchor.

Goodliffe, Jay, and Darren Hawkins. 2006. "Explaining Commitment: States and the Convention against Torture." *Journal of Politics* 68(2):358–71.

Goodliffe, Jay, Darren Hawkins, Christine Horne, and Dan Nielson. 2008. "Norm Enforcement, Dependence Networks, and the International Criminal Court." Unpublished manuscript.

Gouldner, Alvin W. 1960. "The Norm of Reciprocity: A Preliminary Statement." *American Sociological Review* 25(2):161–78.

Graham, Charles. 2003. "A Model of Norm Development for Computer-mediated Teamwork." *Small Group Research* 34(3):322–52.

Granovetter, Mark S. 1973. "The Strength of Weak Ties." *American Journal of Sociology* 78(6):1360–80.

Gruenfeld, Deborah H., Dacher J. Keltner, and Cameron Anderson. 2003. "The Effects of Power on Those Who Possess It: How Social Structure Can Affect Social Cognition." Pp. 237–61 in *Foundations of Social Cognition*, edited by G. V. Bodenhausen and A. J. Lambert. Mahwah, NJ: Lawrence Erlbaum.

Guler, Isin, Maura F. Guillén, and John Muir MacPherson. 2002. "Global Competition, Institutions, and the Diffusion of Organizational Practices: The International Spread of ISO 9000 Quality Certificates." *Administrative Science Quarterly* 47:207–32.

Habyarimana, James, Macartan Humphreys, Daniel N. Posner, and Jeremy M. Weinstein. 2007. "Why Does Ethnic Diversity Undermine Public Goods Provision?" *American Political Science Review* 101(4):1–17.

Haidt, Jonathan, and Jonathan Baron. 1996. "Social Roles and the Moral Judgement of Acts and Omissions." *European Journal of Social Psychology* 26:201–18.

Haidt, Jonathan, and Jess Graham. 2007. "When Morality Opposes Justice: Conservatives Have Moral Intuitions that Liberals May Not Recognize." *Social Justice Research* 20(1):98–116.

Haidt, Jonathan, Silvia Helena Koller, and Maria G. Dias. 1993. "Affect, Culture, and Morality, or Is It Wrong to Eat Your Dog?" *Journal of Personality and Social Psychology* 65(4):613–28.

Hardin, Russell. 1996. "Trustworthiness." *Ethics* 107(1):26–42.

Harris, Judith Rich. 1999. *The Nurture Assumption*. New York: Touchstone Books.

Harris, Marvin. 1989. *Cows, Pigs, Wars, and Witches: The Riddle of Culture*. New York: Vintage.

Hawkins, Darren. 2004. "Explaining Costly International Institutions: Persuasion and Enforceable Human Rights Norms." *International Studies Quarterly* 48(4):779–804.

Hawthorne, Nathaniel. 1850. *The Scarlet Letter.*

Haynie, Dana L. 2001. "Delinquent Peers Revisited: Does Network Structure Matter?" *American Journal of Sociology* 106(4):1013–57.

Heaton, Tim B., and Sandra Calkins. 1983. "Family Size and Contraceptive Use among Mormons: 1965–1975." *Review of Religious Research* 25(2):102–13.

Hechter, Michael. 1987. *Principles of Group Solidarity.* Berkeley, CA: University of California Press.

Hechter, Michael, and Elizabeth Borland. 2001. "National Self-Determination: The Emergence of an International Norm." Pp. 186–207 in *Social Norms*, edited by Michael Hechter and Karl-Dieter Opp. New York: Russell Sage.

Hechter, Michael, and Karl-Dieter Opp. 2001. "What Have We Learned about the Emergence of Social Norms?" Pp. 394–415 in *Social Norms*, edited by Michael Hechter and Karl-Dieter Opp. New York: Russell Sage.

Heckathorn, Douglas. D. 1988. "Collective Sanctions and the Creation of Prisoner's Dilemma Norms." *American Journal of Sociology* 94:535–62.

———. 1989. "Collective Action and the Second Order Free Rider Problem." *Rationality and Society* 1:78–100.

———. 1990. "Collective Sanctions and Compliance Norms: A Formal Theory of Group-mediated Social Control." *American Sociological Review* 55:366–84.

Henrich, Joseph, Robert Boyd, Samuel Bowles, Colin Camerer, Ernst Fehr, and Herbert Gintis, eds. 2004. *Foundations of Human Sociality.* Oxford: Oxford University Press.

Hirschman, Albert O. 1982. "Rival Interpretations of Market Society: Civilizing, Destructive, or Feeble?" *Journal of Economic Literature* 20(4):1463–84.

Hobbes, Thomas. [1651] 1958. *Leviathan.* Indianapolis: Bobbs-Merrill.

Homans, George C. 1950. *The Human Group.* New York: Harcourt, Brace.

Horne, Christine. 2001a. "Community and the State: The Relationship between Normative and Legal Controls." *European Sociological Review* 16(3):225–43.

———. 2001b. "The Enforcement of Norms: Group Cohesion and Metanorms." *Social Psychology Quarterly* 64(3):253–66.

———. 2004a. "Collective Benefits, Exchange Interests, and Norm Enforcement," *Social Forces* 82(3):1037–62.

———. 2004b. "Values and Evolutionary Psychology." *Sociological Theory* 22(3):477–503.

———. 2007. "Explaining Norm Enforcement," *Rationality and Society* 19(2):139–70.

———. 2008. "Norm Enforcement in Heterogeneous Groups," *Rationality and Society* 20(2):147–72.

Horne, Christine, Chien-fei Chen, Justin Berg, Katie Evermann-Druffel. 2009. "Metanorm Expectations: Determining What to Sanction." *Advances in Group Processes*. Bingley, UK: Emerald Group Publishing.

Horne, Christine, Jessica Paulson, and Denise Anthony. 2008. "Enforcing Norms Through Rewards and Punishments: Illustrations from a College Fraternity." Unpublished manuscript.

Horne, Christine, and John Hoffmann. 2005. "Norms and Neighborhoods: Explaining Variation in Informal Control." Unpublished manuscript.

Hostetler, John A. 1993. *Amish Society*, 4th ed. Baltimore, MD: The Johns Hopkins University Press.

Humboldt, Wilhelm von. [1854] 1969. *The Limits of State Action*. Cambridge: The University Press.

Hunt, Scott A., Robert D. Benford, and David A. Snow. 1994. "Identity Fields: Framing Processes and the Social Construction of Movement Identities." Pp. 185–208 in *New Social Movements: From Ideology to Identity*, edited by Enrique Larana, Hank Johnston, and Joseph R. Gusfield. Philadelphia, PA: Temple University Press.

Hunter, James. 1991. *Culture Wars*. New York: Basic Books.

Igou, Brad. 2007. "Valentine Byler vs. the IRS. "Pay Unto Caesar—The Amish & Social Security." *Amish Country News*. http://www.amishnews.com/amisharticles/amishss.htm (accessed July 22, 2008).

Ishida, Takeshi, and Ellis S. Krauss, eds. 1989. *Democracy in Japan*. Pittsburgh, PA: University of Pittsburgh Press.

Jhering, Rudolph von. 1879. *The Struggle for Law*. Translated from the 5th German edition by J. S. Lalor. Chicago, IL: Callaghan.

Johannessen, Koreen, Carolyn Collins, Peggy Glider, and Beverly Mills-Novoa. 1999. "A Practical Guide to Alcohol Abuse Prevention: A Campus Case Study in Implementing Social Norms and Environmental Management Approaches." Tucson, AZ: The University of Arizona Campus Health Service.

Johnston, Hank, Enrique Larana, and Joseph R. Gusfield. 1994. "Identities, Grievances, and New Social Movements." Pp. 3–35 in *New Social Movements: From Ideology to Identity*, edited by E. Larana, H. Johnson, and J. R. Gusfield. Philadelphia, PA: Temple University Press.

Jones, Harry W. 1969. *The Efficacy of Law*. Evanston, IL: Northwestern University Press.

Jones, Stephen R. G. 1984. *The Economics of Conformism*. Oxford: Blackwell.

Kahan, Daniel M. 1996. "What Do Alternative Sanctions Mean?" *University of Chicago Law Review* 63:591–653.

Kahlenberg, Richard D. 2001. *All Together Now: Creating Middle-class Schools through Public Choice*. Washington, DC: Brookings Institution Press.

Katz, Daniel, and Floyd H. Allport. 1928. *Student Attitudes: A Report of the Syracuse University Research Study*. Syracuse, NY: Craftsman Press.

Katz, Michael L. and Carl Shapiro. 1985. "Network Externalities, Competition, and Compatibility." *American Economic Review* 75(3):424–40.

Kelling, George L., and Catherine M. Coles. 1996. *Fixing Broken Windows: Restoring Order and Reducing Crime in Our Communities*. New York: Free Press.

Kerr, Norbert L. 1995. "Norms in Social Dilemmas." Pp. 31–47 in *Social Dilemmas: Perspectives on Individuals and Groups*. Westport, CT: Praeger.

———. 1999. "Anonymity and Social Control in Social Dilemmas." Pp. 103–19 in *Resolving Social Dilemmas: Dynamic, Structural, and Intergroup Aspects*, edited by Margaret Foddy, Michael Smithson, Sherry Schneider, and Michael Hogg. Philadelphia, PA: Psychology Press.

Kitts, James. 2003. "Egocentric Bias or Information Management? Selective Disclosure and the Social Roots of Norm Misperception." *Social Psychology Quarterly* 66(3):222–37.

———. 2006. "Collective Action, Rival Incentives, and the Emergence of Antisocial Norms." *American Sociological Review* 71(2):235–59.

Knutson, B. 2004. "Sweet Revenge." *Science* 305(5688):1246–47.

Kollock, Peter. 1994. "The Emergence of Exchange Structures: An Experimental Study of Uncertainty, Commitment, and Trust." *American Journal of Sociology* 100(2):313–45.

Koremenos, Barbara, Charles Lipson, and Duncan Snidal. 2001. "The Rational Design of International Institutions." *International Organizations* 55(4):761–99.

Kraybill, Donald B. 1989. *The Riddle of Amish Culture*. Baltimore, MD: The Johns Hopkins University Press.

———, ed. 1993. *The Amish and the State*. Baltimore, MD: The Johns Hopkins University Press.

Kuran, Timur. 1995. *Private Truths, Public Lies: The Social Consequences of Preference Falsification*. Cambridge, MA: Harvard University Press.

Lawler, Edward J., Shane R. Thye, and Jeongkoo Yoon. 2008. "Social Exchange and Micro Social Order." *American Sociological Review* 73(4):519–42.

Lee, Gary R. 1987. "Comparative Perspectives." Pp. 59–80 in *Handbook of Marriage and the Family*, edited by M. B. Sussman and S. K. Steinmetz. New York: Plenum Press.

Levitt, Steven D., and Stephen J. Dubner. 2006. *Freakonomics: A Rogue Economist Explores the Hidden Side of Everything*. New York: Harper Collins.

Little, Alicia. 1899. *Intimate China*. London: Hutchinson and Co.

Lynn, Richard. 1988. *Educational Achievement in Japan.* New York: M. E. Sharpe.

Macauley, Stewart. 1963. "Non-contractual Relations in Business: A Preliminary Study." *American Sociological Review* 28:55–67.

Mackie, Gerry. 1996. "Ending Footbinding and Infibulation: A Convention Account." *American Sociological Review* 61(6):999–1017.

———. 2006. Personal communication. December.

March, James G., and Johan P. Olsen. 1998. "The Institutional Dynamics of International Political Orders." *International Organization* 52(4):943–69.

McAdam, Doug, John D. McCarthy, and Mayer N. Zald. 1996. *Comparative Perspectives on Social Movements: Political Opportunities, Mobilizing Structures, and Cultural Framings.* New York: Cambridge University Press.

McAdams, Richard H. 1997. "The Origin, Development, and Regulation of Norms." *Michigan Law Review* 96(2):338–433.

McFarland, Daniel A. 2001. "Student Resistance: How the Formal and Informal Organization of Classrooms Facilitate Everyday Forms of Student Defiance." *American Journal of Sociology* 107(3):612–78.

McLeod, Jay. 1995. *Ain't No Making It: Aspirations and Attainment in a Low-income Neighborhood.* Boulder, CO: Westview Press.

Meares, Tracey L., and Dan M. Kahan 1998. "Law and (Norms of) Order in the Inner City." *Law and Society Review* 32(4):805–37.

Meyer, John W., John Boli, George M. Thomas, and Francisco M. Ramirez. 1997. "World Society and the Nation-State." *American Journal of Sociology* 103(1):144–81.

Meyer, John W., Francisco O. Ramirez, and Yasemin Nuhoğlu Soysal. 1992. "World Expansion of Mass Education." *Sociology of Education* 65(2): 128–49.

Meyer, John W., and Brian Rowan. 1977. "Institutionalized Organizations: Formal Structure as Myth and Ceremony." *American Journal of Sociology* 83(2):340–63.

Milgram, Stanley. 1961. "Nationality and Conformity." *Scientific American* 205(6):45–51.

Millar, John. 1976. *"Origin of Ranks."* P. 117 in *Social Science and the Ignoble Savage,* Ronald Meek. Cambridge: Cambridge University Press.

Miller, Alan S., and Satoshi Kanazawa. 2007. *Why Beautiful People Have More Daughters.* New York: Perigee Trade.

Molm, Linda D. 1997. *Coercive Power in Social Exchange.* Cambridge: Cambridge University Press.

Molm, Linda, Jessica L. Collett, and David R. Schaefer. 2007. "Building Solidarity through Generalized Exchange: A Theory of Reciprocity." *American Journal of Sociology* 113(1):205–42.

Molm, Linda D., and Karen S. Cook. 1995. "Social Exchange and Exchange Networks." Pp. 209–35 in *Sociological Perspectives on Social Psychology*, edited by Karen S. Cook, Gary Alan Fine, and James S. House. Boston, MA: Allyn and Bacon.

Molm, Linda D., David R. Schaefer, and Jessica L. Collett. 2007. "The Value of Reciprocity." *Social Psychology Quarterly* 70(2):199–217.

Moravcsik, Andrew. 2000. "The Origins of Human Rights Regimes: Democratic Delegation in Postwar Europe." *International Organization* 54(2):217–52.

Mouw, Ted, and Michael Sobel. 2001. "Culture Wars and Opinion Polarization: The Case of Abortion." *American Journal of Sociology* 106(4):913–43.

Murdock, George P., and Douglas R. White. 1969. "Standard Cross-Cultural Sample." *Ethnology* 8: 329–69.

Nielsen, Joyce M. 1978. *Sex in Society: Perspectives on Stratification*. Belmont, CA: Wadsworth.

Obama, Barack. 2005. "Teaching Our Kids in a Twenty-first Century Economy." http:obama.senate.gov/speech (accessed January 7, 2008).

Oliver, Pamela. 1980. "Rewards and Punishments as Selective Incentives for Collective Action: Theoretical Investigations." *American Journal of Sociology* 85(6):1356–75.

Olzak, Susan. 1992. *The Dynamics of Ethnic Competition and Conflict*. Stanford, CA: Stanford University Press.

Öman, Arne, and Susan Mineka. 2001. "Fears, Phobias, and Preparedness: Toward an Evolved Module of Fear and Fear Learning." *Psychological Review* 108(3):483–522.

Opp, Karl-Dieter. 1982. "The Evolutionary Emergence of Norms." *British Journal of Social Psychology* 21:139–49.

Ostrom, Elinor. 1990. *Governing the Commons: The Evolution of Institutions for Collective Action*. Cambridge: Cambridge University Press.

———. 2005. *Understanding Institutional Diversity*. Princeton, NJ: Princeton University Press.

Ostrom, Elinor, Ray Gardner, and James Walker. 1994. *Rules, Games, and Common-pool Resources*. Ann Arbor, MI: University of Michigan Press.

Packer, George. 2006. "The Megacity: A Reporter at Large." *The New Yorker* 82(37):64–75.

Pesendorf, Wolfgang. 1995. "Design, Innovations, and Fashion Cycles." *American Economic Review* 85(4):771–92.

Pettit, Philip. 1993. *The Common Mind: An Essay on Psychology, Society, and Politics*. New York: Oxford University Press.

Phillips, Rick. 1998. "Religious Market Share and Mormon Church Activity." *Sociology of Religion* 59(2):117–30.

———. 2008. *American Mormon Cultures: Latter-day Saints in Zion and Babylon*. New York: New York University Press, under contract.

Pitcher, Brian, Phillip R. Kunz, and Evan T. Peterson. 1974. "Residency Differentials in Mormon Fertility." *Population Studies* 28(1):143–51.

Polanyi, Karl. 1944. *The Great Transformation*. Boston, MA: Beacon Press.

Pollan, Michael. 2006. *The Omnivore's Dilemma: A Natural History of Four Meals*. New York: Penguin Press.

Portes, Alejandro. 1998. "Social Capital: Its Origins and Applications in Modern Sociology." *Annual Review of Sociology* 24:1–24.

Posner, Eric A. 1996a. "The Regulation of Groups: The Influence of Legal and Nonlegal Sanctions on Collective Action." *University of Chicago Law Review* 63(1):133–97.

———. 1996b. "Law, Economics, and Inefficient Norms." *University of Pennsylvania Law Review* 144:1697–1744.

———. 2000. *Law and Social Norms*. Cambridge, MA: Harvard University Press.

Pound, Roscoe. 1917. "The Limits of Effective Legal Action." *International Journal of Ethics* 27:150–67.

Powell, Walter W. 1991. "Expanding the Scope of Institutional Analysis." Pp. 183–203 in *The New Institutionalism in Organizational Analysis*, edited by Walter W. Powell and Paul J. DiMaggio. Chicago, IL: University of Chicago Press.

Prentice, Deborah A., and Dale T. Miller. 1993. "Pluralistic Ignorance and Alcohol Use on Campus." *Journal of Personality and Social Psychology* 64:243–56.

———. 1996. "Pluralistic Ignorance and the Perpetuation of Social Norms by Unwitting Actors." *Advances in Experimental Social Psychology* 28:161–209.

Putnam, Robert D. 1993. *Making Democracy Work: Civic Traditions in Modern Italy*. Princeton, NJ: Princeton University Press.

———. 2000. *Bowling Alone: The Collapse and Revival of American Community*. New York: Touchstone.

Ravitch, Diane. 1995. *National Standards in American Education: A Citizen's Guide*. Washington, DC: The Brookings Institution.

Ridgeway, Cecilia L. 2001. "Inequality, Status, and the Construction of Status Beliefs." Pp. 323–40 in *Handbook of Sociological Theory*, edited by Jonathan H. Turner. New York: Kluwer/Plenum.

"Rise and Fall: Mormon Majority Is Slipping Away." *The Salt Lake Tribune*, July 24, 2005. http://extras.mnginteractive.com/live/media/site297/2005/0726/20050726_101404_ DTTTRB24A10.PDF (accessed June 30, 2008).

Risse, Thomas. 2000. "'Let's Argue!': Communicative Action in World Politics." *International Organization* 54(1):1–39.

Rizzo, Thomas A. 1989. *Friendship Development among Children in School.* Norwood, NJ: Ablex.

Rohlen, Thomas P. 1983. *Japan's High Schools.* Berkeley, CA: University of California Press.

Rosenbaum, James E., and Takehiko Kariya. 1989. "From High School to Work: Market and Institutional Mechanisms in Japan." *American Journal of Sociology* 94(6):1334–65.

———. 1991. "Do School Achievements Affect the Early Jobs of High School Graduates in the United States and Japan?" *Sociology of Education* 64:78–95.

Rosenberg, Gerald N. 1991. *The Hollow Hope: Can Courts Bring about Social Change?* Chicago, IL: University of Chicago Press.

Rozin, Paul, Laura Lowery, Sumio Imada, and Jonathan Haidt. 1999. "The CAD Triad Hypothesis: A Mapping between Three Moral Codes (Community, Autonomy, Divinity)." *Journal of Personality and Social Psychology* 76(4):574–85.

Rydgren, Jens. 2007. "The Power of the Past: A Contribution to a Cognitive Sociology of Ethnic Conflict." *Sociological Theory* 25(3):225–44.

Sacks, Jonathan. 1999. *Morals and Markets.* London: Institute of Economic Affairs.

Sampson, Robert J. 2000. "Whither the Sociological Study of Crime?" *Annual Review of Sociology* 26:711–14.

Sampson, Robert J., and W. Byron Groves. 1989. "Community Structure and Crime: Testing Social Disorganization Theory." *American Journal of Sociology* 94(4):774–802.

Sampson, Robert J., Stephen W. Raudenbush, and Felton Earls. 1997. "Neighborhoods and Violent Crime: A Multilevel Study of Collective Efficacy." *Science* 277(5328):918–24.

Schachter, Stanley. 1951. "Deviation, Rejection, and Communication." *Journal of Abnormal Social Psychology* 46:190–207.

Schelling, Thomas C. 1978. *Micromotives and Macrobehavior.* New York: W. W. Norton.

Schneiberg, Marc. 2007. Personal communication.

Schneiberg, Marc, and Elisabeth Clemens. 2006. "The Typical Tools for the Job: Research Strategies in Institutional Analysis." *Sociological Theory* 24(3):195–227.

Schwartz, Richard D., and James C. Miller. 1964. "Legal Evolution and Societal Complexity." *American Journal of Sociology* 70(2):159–69.

Scott, W. Richard. 1995. *Institutions and Organizations*. Thousand Oaks, CA: Sage Publications.

Sell, Jane, and Yeongi Son. 1997. "Comparing Public Goods with Common Pool Resources: Three Experiments." *Social Psychology Quarterly* 60: 118–37.

Sheffrin, Steven M., and Robert K. Triest. 1992. "Can Brute Deterrence Backfire? Perceptions and Attitudes in Taxpayer Compliance." Pp. 143–218 in *Why People Pay Taxes: Tax Compliance and Enforcement*, edited by J. Slemrod. Ann Arbor, MI: University of Michigan Press.

Sherif, Muzafer. 1936. *The Psychology of Social Norms*. New York: Harper and Row.

Sherif, Muzafer, O. J. Harvey, B. Jack White, William R. Hood, and Carolyn W. Sherif. 1988. *The Robbers Cave Experiment: Intergroup Conflict and Cooperation*. Middleton, CT: Wesleyan University Press.

Simmel, Georg. 1955. *Conflict and the Web of Group Affiliations*. New York: Free Press.

———. 1957. "Fashion." *American Journal of Sociology* 62(6):541–58.

Smith, Adam. [1776] 2003. *The Wealth of Nations*. New York: Bantam Classics.

Stark, Rodney, Roger Finke, and Laurence R. Iannaccone. 1995. "Pluralism and Piety: England and Wales, 1851." *Journal for the Scientific Study of Religion* 34(4):431–440.

Stark, Rodney, and James C. McCann. 1993. "Market Forces and Catholic Commitment: Exploring the New Paradigm." *Journal for the Scientific Study of Religion* 32(2):111–24.

Sweeney, Megan M. 2002. "Two Decades of Family Change: The Shifting Economic Foundations of Marriage." *American Sociological Review* 67:132–-47.

Tajfel, Henri. 1982. "Social Psychology of Intergroup Relations." *Annual Review of Psychology* 33:1–39.

Tajfel, Henri, Michael G. Billig, R. F. Bundy, and C. Flament, 1971. "Social Categorization and Intergroup Behavior." *European Journal of Social Psychology* 1(2):149–78.

Taylor, Michael. 1987. *The Possibility of Cooperation*. New York: Cambridge University Press.

Thomas, George M., and Pat Lauderdale. 1988. "State Authority and National Welfare Programs in the World System Context." *Sociological Forum* 3(3):383–98.

Tocqueville, Alexis de. [1835, 1840] 2000. *Democracy in America*. Chicago, IL: University of Chicago Press.

Turner, John C., Rupert J. Brown, and Henri Tajfel. 1979. "Social Comparison and Group Interest in Ingroup Favouritism." *European Journal of Social Psychology* 9:187–204.

Turner, John C., Michael A. Hogg, Penelope J. Oaks, Stephen D. Reicher, and Margaret S. Wetherell. 1987. *Rediscovering the Social Group: A Self-categorization Theory*. Oxford: Blackwell.

Ullmann-Margalit, Edna. 1977. *The Emergence of Norms*. Oxford: Clarendon Press.

van Dijk, Eric, and Henk Wilke. 1995. "Coordination Rules in Asymmetric Social Dilemmas: A Comparison between Public Good Dilemmas and Resource Dilemmas." *Journal of Experimental Social Psychology* 31:1–27.

Ward, Colin. 1973. *Anarchy in Action*. London: George Allen and Unwin.

Webster, Murray, Jr., and James E. Driskell, Jr. 1978. "Status Generalization: A Review and Some New Data." *American Sociological Review* 43:220–-36.

Webster, Murray, Jr., and Jane Sell. 2007. "Why Do Experiments?" Pp. 5–23 in *Laboratory Experiments in the Social Sciences*, edited by Murray Webster, Jr., and Jane Sell. Boston, MA: Elsevier.

Willer, Robb, Ko Kuwabara, and Michael W. Macy. 2006. "The Emperor's Dilemma II: False Enforcement of Unpopular Norms." Unpublished manuscript.

Willer, David, and Henry Walker. 2007. *Building Experiments: Testing Social Theory*. Stanford, CA: Stanford University Press.

Willis, Paul E. 1981. *Learning to Labour: How Working-class Kids Get Working-class Jobs*. New York: Columbia University Press.

Wilson, James Q., and George Kelling. 1982. "The Police and Neighborhood Safety: Broken Windows." *The Atlantic Monthly* 127:29–38.

Wilson, William Julius. 1987. *The Truly Disadvantaged: The Inner City, the Underclass, and Public Policy*. Chicago, IL: University of Chicago Press.

Yamagishi, Toshio. 1986. "The Provision of a Sanctioning System as a Public Good." *Journal of Personality and Social Psychology* 51(1):110–16.

———. 1988. "Seriousness of Social Dilemmas and the Provision of a Sanctioning System." *Social Psychology Quarterly* 51(1):32–42.

Yamagishi, Toshio, Karen S. Cook, and Motoki Watabe. 1998. "Uncertainty, Trust, and Commitment Formation in the United States and Japan." *American Journal of Sociology* 104(1):165–94.

Young, Lawrence A. 1994. "Confronting Turbulent Environs: Issues in the Organizational Growth and Globalization of Mormonism." Pp. 43–63 in *Contemporary Mormonism: Social Science Perspectives*, edited by Marie Cornwall,

Tim B. Heaton, and Lawrence A. Young. Urbana, IL: University of Illinois Press.

Zelditch, Morris, Jr. 1969. "Can You Really Study an Army in the Laboratory?" Pp. 528–39 in *A Sociological Reader on Complex Organizations*, edited by A. Etzioni. New York: Holt, Rinehart, and Winston.

Zimbardo, Philip. 2008. *The Lucifer Effect: Understanding How Good People Turn Evil*. New York: Random House.

Index